Stories
from the
Streets
and beyond

BY JIM REA

DEDICATION

This book is dedicated to the memory of
Sydney Callaghan
Margaret Ferguson
and Helen (Montgomery) McMullan
who in their own unique way brought the gospel to the streets.
They are now in the Father's House.

*All proceeds from the sale of this book
after production and distribution costs
will be donated to two homeless charities:*
**The Welcome Organisation &
Hosford House - East Belfast**

DESIGN • PRINT • PUBLISHING • DISTRIBUTION

Designed & Published by Cedric Wilson
Email: cedricwilson@live.co.uk

FOREWORD

Norman Wisdom and Jim Rea at the Palace

I found this book very easy to read and very enjoyable. The reason is that it is full of stories, and Jim Rea is a great storyteller. He also loves a laugh, so you will find humour in these pages. At the same time many of the stories are deeply moving and might bring a tear to your eye. All of them make a point which will help you in your relationship with God. One of the beauties of the book is that all of the stories stand in their own right. You don't need to have a lot of time available. Just reading one story will be a blessing to you. May you enjoy reading this book, and be inspired by the wisdom that comes from every page

Brother David Jardine

CONTENTS

CONTENTS

HILDA'S PRAYERS AND AN OBSTETRICIAN'S SKILL

In April 1945 an end to war in Europe was in sight. The streets of Belfast were littered with the evidence of German bombing. In the month of April a young woman of twenty two years of age lay seriously ill in the Royal Maternity Hospital. Her young husband was told that their baby was certainly dead and that it might also be difficult to save the mother's life.

Belfast Blitz - High Street

The young man returned to Ottawa Street in North Belfast where he called to see a woman called Hilda Kennedy. Hilda was a woman of prayer, and so she prayed as the young man knelt alongside her on the floor. When a few hours later he returned to the Hospital he was told by an obstetrician that an emergency Caesarean section had been carried out, and his wife had given birth to a son and both were well. The young man was Billy Rea my father. When I was few weeks old Billy my dad stood with me on the floor of Hilda's house and they prayed that God would use this little child in the work of God's Kingdom. Hilda always believed I might be a preacher, but in my early life I had no such aspirations.

My mother was Margaret but called Peggy. I was to spend my early years growing up in Ottawa Street under the shadows of the great mills of North Belfast where much of the linen industry was centred, and where a basic living was eked out by the men and women of that area who lived on the breadline and were treated badly by their employers.

I vividly recall the cobbled street, the two up two down houses with outside toilets and the air raid shelters. We often played in those dangerous air raid shelters before their demolition.

Memories of the war were still vivid in the minds of my parents. They would talk about the two terrible

Grandmother and Hilda

nights of German bombing over Belfast. Stories of death and destruction were common. Blitzed ground would be seen all over parts of North Belfast - these would soon become the domain of tent missions largely conducted by evangelists from the Plymouth Brethren, like Frank Knox who hailed from Cootehill in Co. Cavan. The stories about this man's straightforward style were legendary. My grandmother told me he had been a big card player and that he shuffled the Bible like a pack of cards. He was full of puns, and on a Sunday afternoon he would address the tent goers with "You are full of roast beef and unbelief." At some remarks he made a couple of lads giggle. He looked down at them and sternly waved his finger shouting, "Boys, this is serious!" North Belfast was littered with Mission Halls of very different kinds.

My first experience of Sunday School was at Disraeli St Mission Hall. It was run by two men, Mr Martin senior and his son Herbie. The Mission Hall had connections with Woodvale Presbyterian Church which was nearby, but the hall catered for the working class factory workers who lived in the locality. In the Sunday School I was taught by a nice lady called Mrs Hall, who I think was a daughter of Mr Martin. At night I would go with my father to the Hall for "the meetin": this would be conducted by all sorts of people. There were rough working men whose testimonies were always pretty graphic, and whose sins of the past often brought shock to the hearers. There would always be good gospel hymns from Redemption Hymnal, and often a soloist who was not always easy on the ear, and of course a sermon from a wide variety of preachers. This kind of fellowship gave to people a sense of worth and esteem not found in the factories or the neighbourhood.

Unlike today's society we went in our Sunday best. It was humble and pretty poor but it gave to many a sense of value and belonging. I still have vivid memories of it all. I never regret having experienced it.

And most of all I remember that wonderful Christian woman, Hilda Kennedy, whose prayers for the skills of that obstetrician were answered. Later as a student for the ministry in 1969, when he was giving a lecture on medical ethics, I had an opportunity to thank this amazingly gracious surgeon. He gave my father good news that day and made this book a reality. He would ultimately hold the chair at Queen's University in gynaecology and obstetrics. Professor Jack Pinkerton, a world leader in his field, also became a generous supporter of the East Belfast Mission.

Professor Jack Pinkerton

THE LASTING MEMORY

William was born in the back streets of North Belfast at the end of World War 2. His early life was to witness the ravages of German bombing over Belfast. Life was hard. Men got drunk at the weekends and staggered down the street to their hard-done-by wives. People from both sides of the community, Catholics and Protestants, shared one common experience: they were poor and lived in sub-standard housing.

William's parents went to the local street-corner Mission Hall. The young lad didn't value education much, and left school at fifteen to take up a job. Moving to a new home in a council estate in the early 1950s, life improved. He was deeply challenged after a watchnight service taken by an Elim minister, Yorkshireman Pastor Harry Toft, and so he became a Christian.

Some of young William's friends drifted away, but then he met a new one. Jack was the son of his mother's cousin. A casual meeting included an invitation to Shankill Methodist Church with the promise, "I will meet you outside and sit beside you." How important that proved to be!

This was just a beginning. Later another minister came into his

William aged 3

life, who was also called William. This William was a Dubliner, who came and lived in the working class streets of the Shankill Road. He gave away his money to the poor. He allowed unusual people to live in his home, and used his car as a free taxi for locals in emergencies. Although a non-drinker he went into the local pubs and talked to the working men. He valued and cared for every person he met, and advocated the importance of Christian commitment. It was attractive, practical Christianity. While he was an evangelist, he didn't present the insincerity of prosperity that was often perceived by the locals about some preachers of the day.

He started a class to train young people to become preachers. Young William joined that class. Could he be a minister... not really? His mother told him that ministers were usually the sons of wealthy people, who had failed to be doctors. The minister's neighbour Jinnie, an unusual chain-smoking, rotund lady, who did his housework and called herself a heretic, reinforced William's mother's view, saying that the ministry was a good job for the delicate sons of the rich and prosperous. The minister friend didn't give up on the young fellow, who felt the call of God, and in 1967 William entered training for the Methodist ministry.

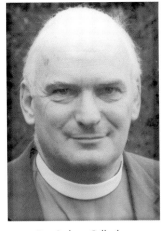

Rev Sydney Callaghan

So we have the story of two men who shared a Christian name, but were never known by that name: one, William Sydney Callaghan. Sydney, as he was known, was the minister who touched the lives of countless people. He ended his earthly life in 2001. As for William James Rea, it is, as you may have guessed, yours truly, this Jim Rea.

Jim and fellow colleagues Ordination Bangor 1973

MANSIONS, NOT ROOMS!

I remember with affection my childhood days when for a time I attended a Gospel Hall Sunday School in Ligoniel, North Belfast, where the members of the Hall dressed soberly and had a rather strict lifestyle. I went with my mates, having heard they gave out sweets for answering questions on the Bible. To my pride, after some time, I received a very classy leather-covered copy of the King James Authorised Version of the Bible for good attendance. From this version we were taught Bible stories and key memory verses of Scripture. To this day what I was taught to recite as a child remains logged in my memory and has regularly proved invaluable in all kinds of contexts, especially when I am preaching.

Jim aged 10

It was only in my late teens that I was introduced to modern translations of Scripture. At the time, with my limited education, I found them helpful and easier to read. But I was soon to discover that in the Belfast Christian community of the 1960s the translation of the Bible one chose to read could become a matter for heated discussion. It is now reckoned that there are well over four hundred different versions of the Bible produced in the English language.

The King James Authorised Version was first produced in 1611, and we must remember that this version, like its many successors, is a translation from Hebrew and Greek manuscripts with reference at times to other ancient languages. As intended, this was to become the people's Bible and also the preachers'. I like to think of John Wesley and George Whitefield using it as they preached in the open-air to thousands during the 18th Century Methodist revival.

But, for me, sentiment will never let me forget that the A.V. was my father's Bible. Whatever translation he read, he never got away from this one. I recall his objection to those ministers who would read modern translations at funerals, especially John chapter 14 verse 2: 'In my Father's house are many rooms.' He would recall a funny story from his impoverished days of the 1930s and then recite an old Belfast rhyme: 'I got married and I met my doom and now we live in an oul back room'. He would retort, 'I'm not going to heaven for a room." It is said that the translators of the Authorised Version took the liberty to use the word 'mansion' to suggest the grandeur of heaven, while the word in the original language suggests 'rooms' or 'dwelling places'. My Dad had a point! Which translation of the Bible is best will always remain a matter for debate, but what will never be disputed is what a wonderful gift this particular version of the Bible is and has been to the English-speaking world with its grandeur and poetic language!

Jim's father Billy Rea

I once conducted a funeral of a man who didn't go to church very often. This man's daughter remarked, "My father dipped into the Bible." I thought to myself that it was no bad thing. Many have 'dipped into' the Word of God, whatever translation, and have made the greatest discovery of their lives: they have found their salvation through a God who forgives sin, the Son of God who died and rose again and ever lives to give us real purpose here and a home in heaven in the hereafter. Not to offend my late father, I should say, 'a mansion'!

UNSUNG HEROES OF THE 1980s

Tommy Coey with Jim Rea at start of Day Centre 1981

My father always reminded me that life is full of unsung heroes. He would often point to a successful person with the added remark, "Did you know who got them there?" Many people got me "there", but I write especially of those who were around my life in the 1980s.

It is true of life that while some people get public plaudits for what they do, others are sometimes ignored. Hence this story. On 23rd November 1985 I became the founder of the East Belfast Mission at its official opening. History will tell you that this was not an easy day in Belfast, because it was the official protest against the Anglo-Irish Agreement. Roads were blocked and traffic diverted, but we filled the Newtownards Road Methodist Church to overflowing. The Mission is now easily recognised by the large development on the Newtownards

John Carson Lord Mayor, Major Cameron Bavis Salvation Army, Martha Carson, Rev Jim Rea, Rev Hamilton Skillen, Rev Billy Peden, Muriel Skillen, Rev Doc Norman Taggart, Archdeacon W.A. Macourt

Road called the Skainos Centre. Sometimes I get people reminding me of my role in the area where I worked for twenty-one years. However, I am always conscious of my need to divert the pats on the back in another direction and remember my father's words.

In 1978 when I became minister of what was then Newtownards Road Methodist Church, Tommy Coey was a regular on a Sunday morning. He always gave me a warm handshake on leaving the church, but I noticed nothing

Early Days of Drop in Day Centre at East Belfast Mission

remarkable about him. It was in May 1980 that I received a call from his wife Kathleen. "Jim, would you go and see Tommy, he's in hospital." "Which one?" I asked. "You don't know this, but Tommy is an alcoholic." I was a bit shocked, but determined to go and see him. I still recall that sunny Sunday evening visiting him in the psychiatric unit. Tommy looked a broken man. He told me about his former life, his heavy drinking and the DIY business burnt out by local paramilitaries because he wouldn't pay them protection money. He shared how earlier in life he

Helen McMullan & Sandra Crooks collecting for E Belfast Mission

made a profession to follow Christ, but he had certainly lost his way. He invited me to pray so that he could ask God for forgiveness and transformation from his addiction.

When Tommy was discharged from hospital, he shared with me his vision. "I own a catering business and I could open a drop-in centre in the church. I will do it voluntarily." I asked some of our leaders and they were very cautious. I did hear, "You don't know what you're letting yourself in for." But Tommy believed in a committee of three with two absent. He pushed on, and on 11th January 1981 our Drop In Centre opened. Helpers and volunteers turned up from everywhere. No scores on the doors, a kitchen that would never pass today's health and safety, but there it was, potatoes, beans and sausages 40p! It took off, people flocked in six days a week. Many of the customers had real issues in their lives. Tommy was a witness to the power of the gospel. Until the day he died, he never drank again. When often asked by former accomplices, "Are you off the drink?" he would retort, "Drinking the new wine of the Spirit!"

Tommy ran a prayer meeting at his home. We needed someone to keep the books and pay bills of the fledgling Day Centre. He introduced me to Sandra (English) McVeigh. She became a woman with incredible ability and energy. When we opened officially as the East Belfast Mission In 1985, Sandra was employed as our Mission Secretary. Not only was she efficient, but she had lots of ideas as to how the mission could expand. She worked tirelessly for its future, even through serious illness.

Francis Moffitt, Sandra McVeigh and Buddy Kirwan

Frances Moffitt could be described as a remarkable woman too. Growing up in South Belfast she was nurtured in Ballynafeigh Methodist Church. During those early years, Frances came into a living faith in Jesus Christ. On leaving school she initially became a civil servant, but ultimately went to work in Whiteabbey Girls' School where she became matron. Through her life many of the young women she cared for, in what was a school for correction, would reconnect with her, confirming the amazing impact she made on their lives. Frances was a dainty lady with an irrepressible spirit. Her sense of right and wrong would dominate her strongly held Christian principles.

The abiding memory of the writer was the contribution she made to the establishment of the fledgling East Belfast Mission. I still recall the day she sat in my office and declared "I have retired at 55." She was offering her services as a volunteer, and was to become secretary of the Mission's Management Committee. A humorous memory is the day when a well-known business on Newtownards Road was refurbishing. They offered the contents of the old office to the Mission. This included chairs and desks. A handcart was procured and along with the writer, Frances was seen pushing it piled high as we wheeled it down the

Jim, Henry Bannister (Project Leader) with Prince Charles at Homework Club

Newtownards Road, to the amusement of the passers-by. The work she did for the East Belfast Mission was immense, as was her wisdom and integrity. She gave her life in reaching out to the marginalised and the poor.

Then there was Helen (Montgomery) McMullan. I recall sitting in our day centre with a student minister from England who was on a placement with me for the summer. I was showing people around who were prospective candidates for a post as a pastoral assistant. He noticed one young woman who freely mixed with the customers as they sat enjoying their lunch. He looked at me and in his broad Lancastrian accent he remarked, "Oh, there's a shine about her!" His judgement was absolutely right. Coming from a Salvation Army background and trained with the Faith Mission, what was the shine? It was the radiance of Jesus Christ, something she brought to every home from the poorest to the richest. Leaving the mission, she married Ben McMullan and they had seven happy years together before she was called home to be with her Lord. Helen was ably succeeded by June Parke who later became a Methodist minister.

There are so many others and some are mentioned elsewhere in this book. But I should add, there was the Rev. Trevor Kennedy before me and Joe Warke who worked every night for many years to keep young people off the streets. Youth leaders John Gowdy, Harry and Carole Nesbitt, who arranged exchange trips with teenagers from the Newtownards Road, Short Strand and west Belfast to America for many years. Robert Reynolds our football coach par excellence. And John and Lilian Watt and Jackie Dawson, Patricia Thompson, Lillian Wilson who impacted the lives of endless young people. Only time will tell the number of young people these good people kept out of paramilitary organisations and influenced for good. Jimmy McKnight and George and Sybil Megahey were prayer warriors who kept our spirits up when thing were tough.

Then there was "Hosford" - that's how he answered the phone. William J. Hosford was a Co Waterford man, a man of prayer and a visionary. Struck by polio in early life which caused him a degree of handicap, he had been a joiner/ cabinetmaker in Harland and Wolff, a magnificent craftsman who went on to be an insurance agent. He had a vision to get people off the streets and to deal with alcohol addiction. He died in his nineties. He was one of

W J Hosford with Annie and Jim McKnight

the greatest Christians I ever met. Hosford House stands in his honour.

Truly the half will never be known. Lives that embraced the Methodist emphasis on evangelism, social justice and personal holiness and could be summed up in the words attributed to John Wesley, "Do all the good you can. By all the means you can. At all the times you can. To all the people you can, as long as ever you can."

Some of them have gone home now to the Father's House, and there are so many others, too many to mention, so that I have restricted my thoughts to those early volunteers. Some others are mentioned elsewhere in this book - they should have the credit for those days of the beginnings of the East Belfast Mission in the 1980s. And they all would say, "To God be the Glory!"

IT HELPED MY GRANNY BREATHE!

Holding up the 'windy'

One of my friends Roy, now a Methodist minister, tells a hilarious story of his early days working in Sandy Row in Belfast. In the local primary school he asked the class this question: "What is the purpose of the Bible?" Quickly a wee lad responded, "Sir," he said, "it's to houl (hold) up the windy (window) to help my granny breathe." Roy confirms that later he walked down the little street where the wee boy lived, only to see, much to his amazement, a wee Bible propping up the window. Every time I recall that story I rock with laughter.

The little boy's remark may sound a bit off the wall but the more I think of it, the more I realise that it was truly profound. Christians often rightly refer to the Bible as the unique word of God. St Paul describes the scriptures in his letter to Timothy as having been God-breathed. Just as the wee lad's ailing granny had to breathe to live, and the open window let in more oxygen, in a different sense scripture is as essential to our spiritual health as the air we breathe.

Its truths inform us about the nature of God and His requirements for a fulfilled life. It reveals God's plan for our salvation and our ultimate destiny, as the result of the coming of Jesus Christ. It provides something amazingly sustaining for the Christian, through the joys and trials of this life. I heard it said recently that we don't read the Bible, it is more that God reads it to us.

It is with this in mind that members of an organisation called the Gideons leave copies of the scriptures in hotels, hospitals, schools and prisons. I have three friends who had incredible experiences with the Bible. One man was a Republican prisoner in Crumlin Road prison when one day he got hold of a copy of the Bible. He tells how its words gripped his attention causing him to pray that the Lord would come into his life. He has spent most of his life since then working with the homeless and sharing his story with people from his Irish Republican background.

My second friend while a young man sadly became a petty criminal. He was sentenced to prison where he found a New Testament supplied by the Gideons in his cell. This too led to a remarkable conversion. Ultimately he became a Baptist minister in the South of England, and then a missionary setting up orphanages in Romania and the Ukraine.

My third friend was a teenager when he absconded from home in the Irish Republic for London where he became a drug user and ultimately lived on the streets. One day with his friends he was rummaging in a bin for food. Remarkably, in the bin someone had dumped a Bible. He often recalls how he carried that Bible in his rucksack everywhere he went as far as North Africa, reading it for comfort in dark moments. On having to return home because of severe illness he was later to experience the transforming power of Jesus Christ. Today he is a Methodist minister.

Sandy Row

What happened to these friends was not that they encountered something they read that was inspirational or a classical piece of literature. They encountered the living word, Jesus Christ in the Bible.

I hope the wee lad's granny found not just help from the Bible that held up a window, but may also have discovered its God-breathed truth in her own life. And so may we, whatever our circumstances are in life.

A SAFE PAIR OF HANDS

Kick-about with Pat Jennings

With the starting of the football Euros my interest in Northern Ireland is reignited. And in a recent game I recall a super save by their young goalkeeper Bailey Peacock-Farrell.

I have always been an admirer of goalkeepers, having tried unsuccessfully to be one. As a little lad we would argue around the question, "Who is the most important player in a football team?" "The centre forward!" somebody would shout. But eventually we would all agree it had to be the goalkeeper, he was the last line of defence.

So you can appreciate how thrilled I was the day I met one of my heroes, Pat Jennings the iconic Northern Ireland goalkeeper. He was just what I expected, a gentleman whose whole demeanour was expressed by his modesty. It was Pat who, on the recent death of the famous Gordon Banks, described Banks as the best goalkeeper of all time. To such a plaudit many football pundits would add Pat Jennings. I had the privilege of watching him playing for Northern Ireland at many of his 119 games. This fine Newry man remains a great role model for all young people playing sport.

What struck me most the day I met him was the size of his hands. I realised it was true, he could catch the ball with one hand!

The regular reference to Pat's 'safe pair of hands' has for me a wider meaning. It was reflected in the characteristics he portrayed in all aspects of his life. This was particularly obvious when he played football. Confidence permeated through the team, a quality we look for in anyone who takes responsibility. Who wants the politician who is cavalier, or the business manager who takes high risks and chances? A safe pair of hands is often required, yet even the best experts in their field make mistakes that are costly. Even the greatest goalkeepers lose vital matches and the best politicians make serious errors of judgement. As we are too aware in recent times, bankers and investors with experience have made disastrous choices.

It was Moses, addressing the tribes of Israel, perhaps foreseeing the turbulent future ahead for his people, who spoke these final words of advice recorded in the Book of Deuteronomy: "The eternal God is your refuge and underneath are the everlasting arms." Later the Psalmist for a moment contemplates the safety of the hills, where his people often took refuge, but then declares that

Jim Rea with Pat Jennings

he doesn't look there, but to the Lord who is his keeper.

It is the promise that if we trust in the God who makes no mistakes, and has our eternal welfare at heart, He will provide our ultimate security, knowing that we are forever in the safest hands, those of the greatest Keeper of all.

ARTHUR WORE THE BEST PERFUME!

Arthur Crozier

When St. Valentine's Day or Christmas comes around, perhaps the more romantically inclined of us will be thinking of possible gift ideas. With flower prices generally going through the roof, perfume never fails to please. Albeit in a world of fakers we have to make sure to get the genuine fragrance, as I discovered once to my embarrassment.

When I think of perfume I don't always think of Calvin Klein, Estée Lauder, or Christian Dior. It's when I think of Arthur. You may we wondering if this is a new designer label. No, Arthur was a Methodist minister.

In 1969 as an inexperienced student minister I went to work with him for part of a summer in Manchester. His church was in Hulme in the middle of a big housing estate where many of the residents seemed to have a multiplicity of problems. In that place, Arthur was always on hand.

On week days, he and I would cycle to Hulme, park our bikes and walk around. We would often call to see the kindly May Lewis. She was disabled and blind and Arthur would put on the tea pot and make us all a cup of tea. After a prayer with May we would leave. Then we might witness a few lads sitting enjoying the sun. Arthur would immediately engage with them. Soon we would know if they were United or City supporters. Around these streets and alleyways Arthur Crozier would invite people to the church with its many activities. On Friday we would go to an iron foundry and have our lunch with the men, mugs of tea and sandwiches eaten off rather dirty tables.

Many of these men bore scars of working in hard conditions and several of them looked years older than they really were. We would hear of all sorts of problems including the fears of redundancy.   Arthur didn't preach, he listened, and then, assuring them of his prayers, he would quietly and sensitively tell them about the God who cared about them more than anyone else could.

So what has this to do with perfume, you might rightly ask? Some years later when I became minister of the East Belfast Mission, I invited Arthur to come to preach at an anniversary weekend. He spoke about some words that St Paul had written, "For we are to God the pleasing aroma of Christ among those who are being saved and those who are perishing." We are the aroma of Christ! The penny dropped - that's what Arthur was! My mind went back to those days in Hulme when I had learned that my friend brought to every conversation the fragrance of Christ. The aroma of the love of God was what made Arthur special. To share that love with all we meet in the months ahead is the best perfume we can ever wear, and well outlasts St Valentine's Day or Christmas Day or any day.

2 Corinthians 2:15 For we are to God the pleasing aroma of Christ among those who are being saved and those who are perishing.

WHO DISCOVERED GEORGE BEST

George Best in action

When the World Cup comes around I often regret that the famous George Best never got the opportunity to play in this competition, as unfortunately Northern Ireland never qualified during his playing days. I had a connection with George, well not really, but rather with the man who discovered him.

History will record that this man was Bob Bishop the famous scout for Manchester United. But what it doesn't say is that in the first instance it was my old friend Stevie Rutherford, who lived in the next street to George on the Cregagh estate.

One day Stevie was watching a young lad playing on the nearby green and was so impressed by his amazing talent that he recommended him to Bob Bishop, and that is how George was ultimately signed for Manchester United. Although Stevie used to tell the story humorously, he never took any credit for spotting George.

When I became minister over 40 years ago of Newtownards Road Methodist Church (now the East Belfast Mission) Stevie was our Boys' Brigade Captain and he had an amazing gift and ability to encourage young boys to play football. He would pay for the pitch, referee the game, characteristically wearing his hat and top coat, with the whistle permanently in his mouth. I would often see him coming off with mud up to his knees and his only suit having to go straight to the cleaners.

The reason he ran football teams and made contact with boys was to influence them for good, because Stevie was absolutely obsessed by his love for Jesus Christ. He completely radiated what he believed. Widely known all over east Belfast as the man with a characteristic greeting, "Yo ho!" and with a laugh that could be heard a mile away, he was loved and respected by all.

Stevie Rutherford

Neither George nor Stevie will be around for future World Cups. I only met George once and that very briefly, but I spent many happy hours with Stevie and his wife Lilian just around the corner from Bestie's birthplace.

This very ordinary east Belfast man has left a mark on my life as one of God's enthusiasts. He sought no fame or fortune, he never valued money, but when good things happened, Stevie's "Praise the Lord!" and Hallelujahs could be heard streets away. Stevie changed footballing history the day he discovered George Best, but it was nothing compared to his greatest discovery of what it meant to love and serve Jesus Christ.

George having a 'wee cup of tea' in East Belfast in the eighties

TERRY WAITE'S AMAZING EXPERIENCE

Ted Edwards

This is the amazing story of two men: one well known to me, the other I only met once. Ted Edwards was brought up in the North of England and was an officer in the Salvation Army. After coming to Ireland he became a Methodist minister.

Ted was a great encourager and I got to know him well. As he grew older he continued to have a great enthusiasm for the gospel. The last years before his "promotion to Glory," as the Salvation Army would say, Ted helped at the Newtownabbey Methodist Mission in Rathcoole.

So what's the link with another man who worked with the Anglican Churches' Church Army? Unlike Ted I only once met Terry Waite, who was in captivity in the Middle East for 1,763 days. One Christmas a friend bought me the latest edition of Terry's book, "Taken on Trust." Terry tells how eventually after some time being held hostage he is given a small radio by his captors. For the first time he connects with the outside world. One day he recalls picking up a church service, on the BBC World Service, from Belfast. He hears the voice of an elderly man praying. Suddenly the man prays, "We pray for all captives and here in Belfast we especially remember Terry Waite and his family." Terry can hardly believe it! "Thank you, old man, whoever you are - I pray for you also..."

I found the story deeply moving. The elderly man was my friend Ted and the Church was the Newtownabbey Methodist Mission. It made me think of the prayers I lead at times in church and say privately, and wonder have they any effect. More often than not, I will never know. For the many people I pray for, I do not know. But then God knows.

Ultimately that prayer was answered when Terry Waite was released. What is not recorded in the book is that after his release, Terry made enquires and found out the name of the man who made the prayer. To his surprise Ted Edwards was contacted by Terry thanking him for the prayer that brought hope and encouragement on that dark day in Beirut.

We can never underestimate the value and effectiveness of our prayers, even when, unlike Ted, we may never know the ultimate outcome.

Terry Waite on a visit to Belfast

A MOTHER'S DAY MEMORY

Grandmother and Grandfather David and Mary McCaughrin

Every Mothering Sunday I remember not only my mother but my grandmother. When I fell out of favour with my mother, there was only one place to go, my granny's wee house just one hundred yards down the street. In the early 1950s, Ottawa Street nestled under the famous linen mills of North Belfast with the scars of German bombing all around. Granny was a warper in Ewarts Linen Mill, I never got my head around what that was. All I knew was that my granny had good friends there, who came from "the other side of the house" as we would say. They worshipped in the big Church on Crumlin Road, called Holy Cross. These were amongst the first women from that religious tradition that I was to meet.

Grandmother and fellow Millworker

I still see those hard wrought women; faces wrinkled drinking tea and entertaining each other with stories from the mills. My granny was a great mimic, taking off to a tee some of the big bosses, causing laughter to rock her wee house. "Treat everybody the same," she would remind me, "have no favourites, God loves them all." As I lay up on her sofa after a school day, I could hear the echoes of Kathleen Ferrier and Joseph Lock on the old gramophone. One could not miss the well-worn Bible sitting close by, whose truths were put into action as she reached out with great kindness in a practical way. It might be a bowl of broth to a sick neighbour or the constant attention given to a local man experiencing terminal illness. I can still remember the tramp who got sandwiches and a hot cup of tea.

1st January 1973 is still indelibly etched in my memory. I was now married and living ninety miles away in County Fermanagh, when my phone rang to reveal the sad news that Granny McCaughrin had died suddenly. I was comforted in my grief by words she often said to me, "Jimmy son, if you trust in the Lord Jesus Christ, you don't fear dying because you're ready."

I sometimes would go back and sit at the bottom of that wee street in North Belfast and tearfully reflect on the memories. Then one day it struck me as I looked at the old house. Two up, two down, no bathroom. I thought, "You know, that place was really a slum." As I drove away that day I reflected again; I thought in that wee house I was taught how to treat my neighbour, irrespective of religious or political differences. I was introduced to classical music and the great hymns of the Christian Church, and even better, there I heard the stories of Jesus for the first time. Surely not, it could never have been a slum! Thanks to my grandmother it is my indelible memory.

KNOWN ONLY TO GOD

Keith Garner

I remember the day well; there he was sitting in my office. Our Mission secretary Sandra said to me, "You will be interested in talking to this guy." He was introduced as Keith and he had come to Northern Ireland for his first visit. He was a Methodist minister working in Darlington and he had good reason to be here, as he explained.

Brought up in the famous Lancashire town of Bolton he was an unruly young lad who did not take much interest in the church, but attended the youth club in nearby Worsley. Fascinated by sport, Keith was a fan of the "Trotters", better known as Bolton Wanderers, and he had a passing interest in Rugby League. So when he heard that Ken Macklin, the famous Rugby League commentator of the 1970s was coming to a sports service at the Methodist church, he was very interested. However, disappointment was to follow, for on the Sunday that Macklin was to come, dense fog hit Lancashire and nothing moved, resulting in the famous man being unable to make the journey. The local minister was grabbing at straws. His brainwave was to ask some lads from down the road at the nearby Padgate Teacher Training College to tell something of their experience of Christ.

As Keith puts it, "One lad was from Northern Ireland, he told his story and it made the difference. I thought about it and the next Sunday I turned up at the Methodist church and I gave my life to Christ. I don't know the name of the lad. I only know he came from Northern Ireland."

And there he was sitting in my office - just hoping that the visit might help us find the man whose story led Keith into a living relationship with Christ. Alas, we've never found him. But Keith grew to love Northern Ireland, returning here many times to preach. He would often say, "I feel I owe the place something."

As for Keith Garner, having worked influential appointments and positions within the British Methodist Church, he is now the minister of the famous Wesley Mission in Sydney, Australia. In a church with an amazing outreach, he now superintends a staff of 3,000. Sometimes when I switch on the God channel I hear him preaching - for he now has a worldwide ministry in teaching and evangelism - but I never see him without thinking that there is a man known only to God and not yet to be found, whose word on a foggy night in Worsley made an impact beyond all comprehension.

THE SHANKILL MAN I REMEMBER

Constable Clements

Billy Clements and his wife Ella emigrated to South Africa in the mid-1950s. I recall that we would often remember the family at a prayer meeting in Shankill Methodist Church. I knew Billy's brother Sam from his days in Shankill, and later working together with him in the Methodist ministry. It was in the early 70s that I first met Billy. He and the family had returned to Northern Ireland and he was now working in Portadown. A few years later I got to know him better when working in Co. Fermanagh. On one occasion I attended a prayer meeting in a convent in Omagh and was surprised to find Billy leading the meeting and sharing his knowledge of the Bible with the sisters and the lay people who had gathered. In those days this was engaging in something that would often draw criticism from people who did not share any enthusiasm for contacts with the Roman Catholic community. The Catholic Church in Ireland, now influenced by Vatican II, was encouraging its members to read the Scriptures and to have a greater openness to those in the Protestant community.

Working in both the drapery and shoe trade Billy was always dapper in his dress. He had a broad smile, a warm personality and a faith that radiated from him before he spoke. It was obvious that those attending the convent prayer meeting really loved and respected him. During this period Billy considered that he could further serve his community by joining the RUC Reserve. His fairness, integrity and compassion would be well used in this role.

It was a cold clear Saturday evening on the 7th December 1985. Billy was on duty, having changed his shift with a colleague in order to attend a prayer meeting. I came home that evening to see my wife Carol looking shocked. She said, "I've something very sad to tell you, Billy Clements and his colleague were murdered this evening by the I.R.A. in Ballygawley." I was stunned. "Billy Clements," I thought, "how unjust, he hadn't a sectarian bone in his body." I could only think one thing. He was in heaven.

I attended his funeral service in the little Methodist Church at Ballynanny near Ballygawley where he had served as a local preacher. I was moved by the courage and Christian grace of his wife Ella and the family. I reflected and wondered how any good could come out of this atrocity. A few years later I would come to know Billy's son David, who left his medical career to train for the Methodist ministry. Over the years David's experience of loss has helped countless numbers of people, many of them victims of the troubles. His evangelical faith and his comments in the

Bomb scene Shankill Road

media have been full of insight, and as a local minister he brought first hand comfort to the grieving relatives of the Shankill bomb in October 1993. He has become a Christian leader in his own right. He would be the first to admit that his father's testimony and inspiration have brought to him incredible motivation which makes him someone who doesn't have a theory of loss but has actually experienced it. When I look at David, words of the St Paul come to mind, even though they aren't always easy to understand: "And we know that in all things God works for the good of those who love Him." Often that one man from Shankill comes to mind: Billy Clements who now serves in "the Father's House."

KEEP IT LIT! WITH CHRISTMAS IN MIND.

In our old house in Ottawa Street in north Belfast, I still recall my mother's attempt to light the fire. She carefully screwed up an old newspaper, set the sticks, added a few coals, and then struck a match. She would then stand back and quietly pause. More often than not, nothing would happen. She would wait for a further moment and then she would lift a folded newspaper and vigorously wave it at the fire. Suddenly things began to happen, and a flame would appear. Then sternly she would look at me and say, "Now you must never do that!" An early lesson on health and safety, but not the best example.

This memory came back to me when I read some words in 2 Timothy 1 v 6 in the New International Version, where Paul instructs Timothy to "fan the flame." The context was to keep the memory alive of what God had done in Timothy's life, and an encouragement to draw on his spiritual heritage, from the Christian influence he inherited from his mother and grandmother.

In my experience there is no season of the year when we fan the flame of memory more than Christmas. For many, Christmas is a most difficult time of the year, particularly if the loss of a loved one comes into sharp focus. On the lighter side, our elderly relatives who   use to join us would reminisce around the Christmas dinner. We always had laughter in our home, in the expectation that when my late mother-in-law and father would come on Christmas Day they would inevitably talk about their memories of World War 2 in Belfast. Our children called it "Christmas with Hitler."

More significantly, the Carol Services we might happen to attend, with the traditional scripture readings and carols, may also fan a flame. For in these we are reminded of the nature of God. They tell the story of salvation, the wonder that Jesus is not simply a man of God, but He is the God-man. As St Paul writes, "He is the image and likeness of the invisible God." The eighteenth century Methodist hymnwriter Charles Wesley put it profoundly: "Our God contracted to a span, incomprehensibly made man" - awesome words that may take a moment to digest.

When we hear words from the readings and the carols for the umpteenth time, may they fan a flame and rekindle their amazing message. It could be a transforming moment!

Jim with Mother Peggy and Father Billy at Ottawa Street Belfast

HEAD HEEL OR TOE, SLIP IT TO JOE!

My father introduced me to the name of Joe Bambrick with the rhyme "Head, heel or toe, slip it to Joe." Joe was the Linfield centre-forward whose goal scoring ability was legendary. As we watched some of the greats like Jackie Milburn, Jimmy Greaves or Bobby Charlton, I would be informed that none of them would come close to Joe. My father took delight in informing me that he was present as a thirteen year old who climbed the fence into Celtic Park on the 1st February 1930, to see his hero score six goals when Ireland defeated Wales 7-0. A record that was not broken in international football until sixty-seven years later.

As a little boy I recall seeing Joe. My father pointed him out to me on the Donegall Road. "There's Joe Bambrick," he said, as we stood for a moment in awe. In 1983 I was visiting a patient in the City Hospital who told me that Joe was in a nearby bed. For a few minutes I talked to this shy, quiet man who with his frail hand wrote his autograph on a scrap of paper that I still cherish until the present day. Many older men have confirmed to me the memories of the great man. Often he was described as an opportunist who hung around in the goal mouth and didn't put in a lot of work but seemed to get goals from everywhere. After the famous game with Wales he was chided by the defeated Welsh goalkeeper who with a sense of annoyance complained, "You get six kicks of the ball and you get six goals," the usually shy Bambrick corrected him: "Wait a minute, Taffy, one of them was a header."

Often in my youth I thought of this hero and hoped that maybe someday my goal scoring ability would be recognised, but it was not to be: "useless," "tube," "puddin" could be heard from the sidelines to describe my efforts.

The word goal for me took on a wider meaning. Eventually I would come to understand it differently and even discover that it just didn't appear in football reports but was used several times in the world's best seller, the Bible. The Apostle Paul mentions it on a few occasions: he says, "I have not yet reached my goal, and I am not perfect. But Christ has taken hold of me." Joe scored thousands of goals in his day playing for not only Linfield but Chelsea and Walsall. Those who met him would never have been made aware of his greatness. Such goals we may have never scored, but if we come under the influence of the greatest manager of all and have made Jesus Christ our Lord and Saviour, then we will have scored the greatest goal of all.

Joe Bambrick

"THE FLEGS!"

Some years ago, I was driving through Belfast with my eight year old grandson in the car, when suddenly he pointed, "There's a tricolour!" I paused and then quietly said to him, "Well, it has a good meaning: that green, white and orange really represents peace between the orange and the green traditions living on the island of Ireland." Later as we came closer to home, I pointed to a Union Flag, "It too has a good meaning," I said, "because on it are the three crosses representing the loyalty of St Patrick, St George and St Andrew to Jesus Christ more than anyone else." He listened intently but said nothing.

Some weeks later, he and I were settling down with a bag of sweets to watch the Irish Cup Final between Glentoran and Cliftonville on TV. "There it is again," he pointed at the screen, "the tricolour!" Before I could say a word he went on, "I know, I remember. It means peace between the green and orange, but it will never happen." Oh, I thought, I haven't made much progress. "Well," I said, "we must work to make it happen so that you will have a better future for your generation." "No, it will not happen!" he replied. The mind of my eight year old grandson had been to Sunday

School and went on to make a connection with the story from the Garden of Eden about sin and human failure.

His thoughts were more profound than my initial reaction. How often are the good efforts we make thwarted by the evil deed, or malevolent thought? A friend once remarked to me that no matter how much you try to make peace in this country there's always somebody out to wreck it.

Disturbing it may be, but Granda is not giving up. Not putting aside for one moment the right of people in this community to have strong political allegiances or aspirations, I wonder if we gave first place in our lives to the One whose cross appears on the Union Flag, and whose peace appears on the flag of the Irish Republic, would it make a difference? The first century Christians were Greeks, Jews, Romans and an assortment of others. They may have disagreed on many issues, but they put Jesus Christ first in their lives and it changed the world!

AUNTIE THERESA AND THE FLUTE

James Galway

I got the impression there was something different about my great auntie Theresa. I recall my mother whispering to me that she was "a Catholic." I also realised my granny had a great shine for her. The reason became obvious. My grandmother's brother Harry, who served in the Second World War, had a tragedy hit his life when his wife died, leaving him with three children. Later, Harry remarried and this was Theresa. Not much was said about it, and relationships were always good. Theresa and Harry were to extend their family with a few more children. Granny's admiration was based on how good she was to her step-children.

Every Monday Theresa would arrive in our street to help my grandmother with the washing. A tougher task then than it is today! Knowing her family responsibilities granny would reward her with a few shillings, but there was a problem. I had bought a tin flute   from my pocket money. Although I didn't know about him then, I was soon becoming a budding James Galway. Picking tunes up from the local flute bands, I learned ones that were more highly regarded on the Shankill Road than on the Falls, where they wouldn't have gone down too well. One day as I played a well-known tune to my granny's disdain, she waved her finger at me: "Jimmy, son, that flute will not be here when your auntie Theresa comes up on Monday."

I often reflect on this humorous incident. My grandmother was a devout Christian. She spoke easily of her faith to everyone including Teresa, but she knew what was important, and most of all about respect. There was no way she would offend her lifelong friend. As time went on, it was a lesson I wish had been more widely learned across our community.

Grandmother and great auntie Theresa

CONTRASTING MEMORIES

Titanic Belfast opened in 2012 and is now one of the world's leading visitor centres. Not to be missed if you come this way! When I think of the history of the Titanic and its sinking on April 1912, there are always a few stories I recall.

Major Peuchen was a Canadian army officer and a millionaire. Being a first class passenger, he was enjoying fine food and conversation when he heard that the ship was sinking. Reluctantly he moved towards the lifeboats, but then suddenly returned to his cabin where there was reputed to be 200,000 dollars' worth of cash and shares in the safe. But when he returned a few minutes later, all he had with him was a good luck pin and three oranges. To survive on a life boat in the cold Atlantic an orange might be of greater worth than money.

Belfast shipyard workers

Peuchen did survive. He remained critical of the leadership given on the ship and as a result he made many enemies. He was perceived by the press as one who survived while women and children perished. Later he would face the 1920s Wall Street crash, spending the last years of his life in relative poverty.

In contrast, on the ship that night there was a Scottish minister on his way to take up an appointment at the large Moody Bible Church in Chicago. He was 39 years old, a widower accompanied by his young daughter and another relative. While they survived, Harper didn't. He decided not to put on a life jacket or find a lifeboat, but to preach from the deck to all those around him, urging them to look to Jesus Christ in this moment of crisis. Harper was emphasising his complete confidence in life after death for all who trust in Jesus Christ. One witness confirmed that he eventually dived in the water and continued to preach to those around him. "I am going down. No!" he shouted, "I am going up." Unlike Major Peuchen who survived, Harper's story was not widely known, except that Harper Memorial Baptist Church in Glasgow now stands in his honour. In 1916 in Ontario a young man confessed that after a wayward and careless life, in the dark freezing North Atlantic, he heard the preacher's words. He accepted Jesus Christ as his Saviour and his life was changed forever: "I was John Harper's last convert," he exclaimed. What a lasting memory!

John Harper

TWO CATHOLICS IN THE BAND!

George Henderson

My earliest memories of George are when I met him in Trillick, Co Tyrone, where I went to be a minister in 1972. Living in Irvinestown, Trillick was one of three churches I had the care of. I was a city boy who grew up amidst the linen mills, the iron foundries and the shipbuilding industry of Belfast, so my knowledge of farming could be written on the back of a postage stamp. I knew more about trades than tractors. I soon realised that Belfast caricatures about farmers, such as they were always complaining or had it easy, were a myth. George was a hard working industrious farmer and when I would call, he could be seen in the distant fields sitting on his tractor. I always enjoyed visiting this family; George and I shared a common interest in football and he and Elizabeth had three lovely and lively wee boys. There was sometimes a bonus on the visit. George, as I left, would dump a bag of lovely spuds in the boot of my car, or sometimes a piece of meat from his freezer.

But these reflections are not really my most memorable recollection of this man. What do they say about first impressions? You see the first time I met George, I did not even know he was a leader in the Methodist church. I had only arrived one week when I was to take a service for the local Orange Lodge. Arriving at the church on a sunny July Sunday afternoon, I was approached by this man, still unknown to me, who looked to be a key figure in the Lodge. "Can I speak to you a minute, reverend?" he asked, as he beckoned me down the side of the church. "Will you be saying anything political in your sermon today, or," he went on, "anything about Roman Catholics?" I assured him that my sermon would be a presentation of the gospel in which I would once again offer the message of God's forgiveness and salvation in

Jesus Christ. He smiled, "That's good, I am so relieved. You see there are two Catholic fellows in the band and we would not want to offend them."

If ever I have a memory of George, it will be this one, as it displayed all the incredible qualities of respect and tolerance for people from a different tradition. It came from a man who valued his own background and upbringing.

What is interesting is, that Trillick has been a relatively peaceful town where Orangemen have walked even though in the minority. When Trillick Methodist Church celebrated its 175th anniversary of witness, the event was attended by all sides and George was one of the speakers who welcomed people from near and far. I just wish that George's attitude had been applied by more people in the years of sectarianism and bigotry that followed. Perhaps those good Trillick people had read Romans 13 v 10 "Love does no harm to its neighbour."

BREAD THAT LASTS

I recall hearing a lot about Barney Hughes, often with a few humorous lines. "Barney Hughes' bread sticks to your belly like lead....." I still recall his electric bread-carts humming through the streets of Belfast. Most of all I recall tasting the famous bread on the Falls Road. It sat on my Aunt Kathleen's table. Her dad was an expert baker and as we sat at the table he entertained us with how the bread was made. These were the 1950s. My father's brother Tommy married Kathleen and she was "a Catholic."

In days when this was uncommon and somewhat "persona non grata" we got on well. Often we made our way across the Shankill onto the Falls and nobody said a word. We shared common problems, there wasn't too much money around so a cake was a bit of a rarity, but a Barney's big crusted bap with jam and a bit of laughter did the job, and despite our religious differences we got on well.

When one day I drove down College Street in Belfast I noticed a blue plaque on house No. 11 in memory of Barney Hughes, the famous name in the Belfast I grew up in. Bernard (Barney) Hughes was born in Armagh; starting work as a baker's boy in 1820, he moved to Belfast in 1826. Starting with a small bakery in Church Lane this successful businessman soon expanded and in 1840 he opened his own bakery business in Donegall Street. He was to be quickly recognised as Belfast's leading master baker as he developed his business into the largest baking and milling enterprise in the whole of Ireland.

A man of strong social conscience, Barney became Belfast's first elected Catholic representative on Belfast City Council; all sections in an increasingly divided city respected him. His political and personal courage was characterised by a deep hatred of sectarianism. In the 1850s and 60s he made courageous attempts to defuse the bitter sectarian riots that were developing in Belfast.

Yet for all of that he will be remembered most for the creation of Barney's bap. Realising the poverty and desperate needs of the people of his day, Barney made a bap that was affordable and nourishing, providing a stable diet for the city's poor. He realised the essential nature of bread in keeping people alive.

From the beginning of time bread has been a staple food of life. Significantly it was Jesus Christ who, seeing the needs of the multitude, turned five small loaves and two fishes into enough to feed five thousand. John's gospel records that He went on to say, "I am the bread of life. He who comes to me will never go hungry, and he who believes in me will never be thirsty." This is not to suggest He would satisfy physical hunger or thirst, but more importantly He would offer that which could fulfil and give purpose to the life of every person who desired to know Him.

Barney's bap became an important item on many a table in days of poverty, as it did in that house on the Falls where I still share those memories with my cousin Margaret.

Today bread of many kinds and varieties is in plentiful supply - just look in any supermarket. The bread that Jesus offers satisfies our deepest spiritual hunger but the irony is that it's not always our choice from the menu.

THE STOKER WHO WENT MISSING

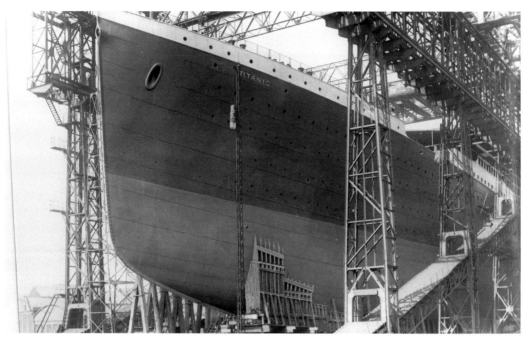

Titanic under construction

In April 2012 I heard a story but wanted to confirm if it was true, and so I went to talk to a lady who lives in the shadow of the giant cranes of the Belfast Shipyard. I heard she had a great story to tell. This lady graphically describes a memory handed down to her by her forbearers. It is about her great grandfather Peter Walsh, who worked over one hundred years ago as a stoker on the Titanic. She recalls how her great grandmother received a telegram from the White Star Line informing her that her husband Peter had been lost at sea. Everyone was in mourning.

However, just a couple of days after the message arrived, something startling happened: into the street came Peter in a jaunting car! The neighbours thought they had seen a ghost, or that Peter had come back from the dead. So what happened? Peter had got off the Titanic at Southampton and had gone into a dockside pub and had a drink or two too many. Then to his dismay he stood on the quay and watched the great ship sail out of the port without him. Earlier he had seen men standing around the docks looking for work. The White Star Line had obviously hired someone else in his place. My friend remarked that it was the only time she could say that Guinness really was good for you!

As she looks at the cranes each day, the story continues to have an impact on her. The person hired that day died in Peter Walsh's place. I witnessed the emotion as this lady told me that in a more profound way, that was what Jesus Christ had done for her on the cross. She explained that this truth came to her as she attended a service in a local church and listened to a sermon on the death of Jesus Christ. She immediately thought of her great grandfather, but somehow saw the difference between his experience and what Christ dying for her really meant. It was her moment of conversion.

For me it was an amazing conversation. Whatever shock Peter Walsh brought to his family and friends on that April day in 1912, he didn't really rise from the dead. Providentially he escaped death and lived until he was a ripe old age. But when Jesus Christ rose, that was different. While He died on the cross and took the punishment for our sins, He rose again and that means that death is now conquered: all who grasp what He accomplished by dying and rising again will discover the promise to those who trust in Him when he said, "Because I live you will live also."

Some of the Titanic stokers

THE MAN IN THE THREE PIECE SUIT

It was as a young lad growing up on the streets of North Belfast that I spotted Robbie for the first time. He was dressed in his three piece suit and an Anthony Eden hat. Walking close behind him were a few lads on their way to Sunday School at the local Methodist Church. I soon began to realise that this was the pattern every Sunday, as he walked from the newly built housing estate where I lived, to the Methodist Church in the village of Ligoniel.

It was some time before I got to know him better. Certainly not dressed in the styles of the 60s youth this amiable warm Christian man looked more like a local solicitor or, professional in his three piece suit bedecked by the gold Albert watch chain hanging from the waistcoat. The traditional style stood out in that relatively poor working class community. Yet he seemed like the Pied Piper for wherever he went young people followed him.

Moving on from that area in my early twenties I lost contact with Robbie but often talked about him. One day in a conversation with another minister I mentioned his name. "Oh," said my friend, "Robbie is great character. I met him one day in a newsagent's in Belfast and there he was buying a motor cycle magazine with a big Norton on the front. I looked somewhat amazed and asked Robbie, 'Are you into motor bikes in big way?' 'No,' was his reply, but I have a boy in my Bible class who thinks about nothing else but motor bikes and I want to try and get into his world.'"

The penny dropped and I understood Robbie's secret. The Book of Proverbs came to mind "Good understanding wins favour." Getting inside the world of the fantasy budding motor cyclist who saw himself lapping the Dundrod Circuit in record time was Robbie's way of making connections.

I recalled that in his Sunday School class he expounded the Bible in a winsome sort of way and listened carefully to the fears and aspirations of his young hearers. He dealt with real problems we were facing in the 1960s. Nothing of the Bible bashing or down your throat style, Robbie spoke quietly with a smile as he commended the way of Jesus Christ to all us.

The passage of time has meant that I have lost contact with many from Robbie's Sunday School class, but I still hear from some of them. What amazes me is that many of them are following Robbie's greatest friend Jesus Christ and are making a real contribution in different parts of the world. On occasions when we meet we will inevitably speak affectionately of the man in the three piece suit who walked the streets of North Belfast on Sunday afternoons and who made Jesus Christ real because he connected in a wonderful way the relevance of the Christian faith by getting inside our world

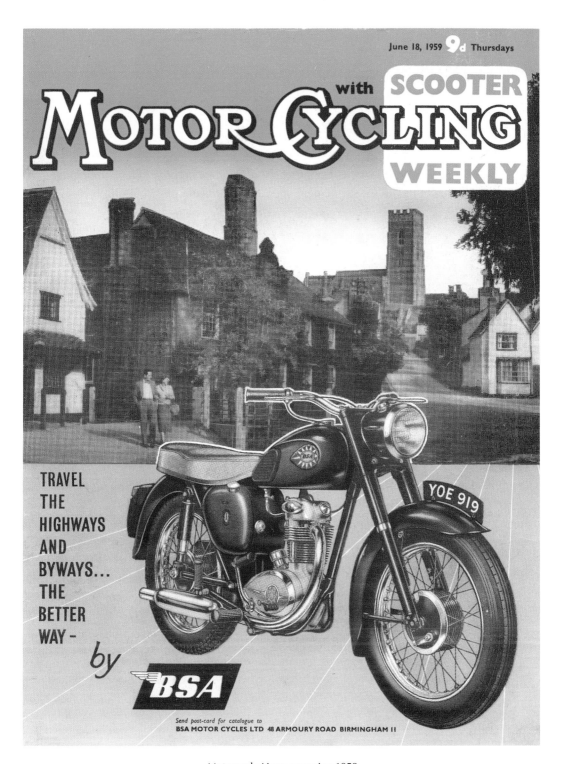

Motorcycle News magazine 1959

MORE TO LIFE THAN FOOTBALL!

When I heard recently of the sacking of a well-known football manager, I recalled a quote from another famous football manager, Bill Shankly. On one occasion on being questioned on the importance of football, Shankly quipped, "Some people believe football is a matter of life and death. I am very disappointed with that attitude. I can assure you it is much, much more important than that." I can still feel myself recoiling at Shankly's words.

I am a football enthusiast, but where has it gone wrong? Someone has said "it's the new religion." I read recently on a website the words of a fan, "Rangers is my religion and Ibrox is my church." A stark reminder that Shankly's famous quote is what many people believe football to be, "more than a matter of life and death." Winning is of the essence, as one adds to that the iniquitous amounts of money that now dominate the game.

Despite that quote I still admired Bill Shankly, a successful manager of Liverpool winning many trophies over fifteen years. But then one day I had a conversation with a minister from Liverpool that made a great impact on me. He knew lots about the club. He told me how after retirement in 1974, Bill Shankly's health deteriorated and to add to his sadness, he no longer felt welcome at Anfield. In fact he had a very low profile around Liverpool, living only for a further seven years.

Bill Shankly

"I was never comfortable with that quote about football being more than a matter of life and death," I said to my friend. "Ah but," he smiled, "did you not know that during the last six months of his life he was visited by an Anglican vicar called Alan Godson. What is not so well known is that in those last months of his life Alan Godson led Bill Shankly to accept Jesus Christ as his Saviour. He died with great confidence and hope." I was deeply moved; Bill Shankly had at last found that there was more to life and death than football. The trophies won would only last for a season, but a personal faith in Jesus would last forever. "Make sure to tell that story," said my minister friend as we said goodbye. I now understood why they sang Amazing Grace at his memorial service in Liverpool's Anglican Cathedral.

Another win

NO FORGIVENESS

As a very inexperienced young minister, one day I encountered a daunting problem. When visiting an elderly lady she told me that in her past life she had committed a sin and felt she could never be forgiven. Troubled by her comments I continued to make visits to her home, never to convince her that she could experience forgiveness. She never told me what the issue in the past was, nor did I feel it appropriate to probe any further. Sadly in the years I knew her she could never find any sense of peace.

What I was not ready for, was that in the years ahead I would meet this problem time and time again. The onset of the troubles in Northern Ireland, and the things that had happened to many people, brought further barriers for many to experiencing peace and forgiveness.

In contrast I recall a phone call from a young woman. I knew something of her troubled past and how difficult she found the memories of it. "I have discovered it!" she exclaimed "God really loves me and has forgiven me." The joy and relief in her voice remains in my memory.

What I have concluded from these contrasting experiences is that some people, while in theory knowing that God can forgive them, cannot forgive themselves.

It is fair to say that the Christian message on forgiveness turns human logic upside down. Logic suggests you need to pay something back in order to be forgiven. You need to take some punishment. Rightly those who break the civil law have to receive justice, or society would end up in anarchy. However God is different. Christ's death on the cross is God's amazing way of taking our sin onto Himself. The nineteenth century hymn writer Fanny Crosby in the popular hymn "To God be the Glory" writes in one line, "The vilest offender who truly believes, that moment from Jesus a pardon receives."

Now we should never be comfortable when people say somewhat glibly, "Oh God has forgiven me." I have heard this sentiment and it can sound trite. We should never minimise sin and wrong doing. However if we genuinely repent before God we can be forgiven. Confession and repentance, followed by the evidence of a changed life, are the hallmarks of a true Christian experience. The writer John says, "If we confess our sins, He is faithful and righteous to forgive us our sins and to cleanse us from all unrighteousness." 1 John 1:9. Whether that elderly lady ever found forgiveness and peace with God, I will never know. But if she had asked for it, she would have received it, even if she never felt it.

Fanny Crosby

O perfect redemption, the purchase of blood!
To ev'ry believer the promise of God;
the vilest offender who truly believes,
that moment from Jesus forgiveness receives.

THE HUMAN CORKSCREW

Harry Toft was a pastor at the Pentecostal Church where I grew up in Ballysillan, North Belfast. Harry was an impressive man. He had an incredible radiance about him. I still remember him as a man who had little concern for material things. He lived with his wife and son a very simple lifestyle in a small house in North Belfast. When Harry left North Belfast in 1967 he went to work as pastor in the South of England, but there he died a few years later at the comparatively young age of 61. Harry Toft was a good advert for Christianity, but it was some of the stories he told that I still remember. He would often speak about his father who had lived a troubled life, but had the great honour of representing Swansea in Rugby Union. He played fly half and sometimes centre, and was widely known for his nickname "The Human Corkscrew". He claimed his greatest moment was when playing for Swansea and beating Australia on Boxing Day 1908 in front of forty thousand roaring fans. For years the people of his home town Swansea would recall the moment to him and shake his hand. Ultimately, to get a living, Harry made the unpopular choice with the Rugby Union authorities and signed for a Rugby League Club in Leeds, where Harry (jun.) was brought up.

During these years at Leeds, something traumatic happened to Harry's father, when he was stricken with cancer with a terrible prognosis. But it was not to be the end, God intervened and he had a miraculous recovery which he claimed to be a miracle. He often spoke of how wherever his father would go telling his story of restoration and healing, people's lives would be changed.

Then Pastor Harry would often finish the story of his father's life, with something incredibly poignant. He would graphically tell of going to his father's bedside as his

life came to an end. He was now seventy-seven years old and was dying but he had something important to say: "Harry," he would point, "I used to think that the greatest moment of my life was the day when we beat Australia, but Harry, I tell you, the greatest day of my life was when I met with Jesus Christ."

Swansea RFC 1st XV 1908-09 Season Back Row(L to R): Bob Dowdle (Trainer), F E Gordon, H Thomas, G Hayward, E Morgan, D J Thomas, D Davies, A Smith, F E Perkins (Sec.). 2nd Row(L to R): I Morgan, F Lewis, J Bancroft, W J Trew (C), P Hopkins, H Hunt, D Griffiths. Front Row(L to R): R M Owen, H Toft, R H Jones.

I will never forget the tremendous impression that story made on me. I was in my teens and very compelled by sport. I thought Christianity was a dull business and there was much more out there to give satisfaction, but that story made a difference to my perspective. Not immediately on hearing it, but I too have found it my life's greatest reality. The greatest day of my life was the day I met with Jesus Christ. When after a Watchnight Service on 31st December 1959 when the Human Corkscrew's son Harry Toft was the preacher.

Wallaby Haka 1908

I WILL RETURN" - IDLE WORDS OR FOR REAL?

In my boyhood days, having a scrap with a mate in a school playground was no unusual thing. I think it gave me and my school pals our early interest in boxing. The names of Joe Lewis, Rocky Marciano, Sonny Liston were in everyday conversation. However, the emergence of Cassius Clay, who later became known as Muhammad Ali, was unique in the boxing world. His arrogance and style, with the catch-phrase "I am the greatest," impressed some but antagonised many. However he was unquestionably the greatest boxer of the era. Known for his gimmickry and humorous verses, "I like your company and I like your style, but I have to leave you after a while," "Float like a butterfly, sting like a bee, his hands can't hit what his eyes can't see" were often quoted. I was in my teenage years and recall turning on my bedside radio at 3.00am in the morning of the 26th February 1964 to hear the commentary of the fight in which he won against the 'unbeatable' Sonny Liston. World heavyweight boxing had changed forever, as Ali with his unique style defended his world crown on numerous occasions in a career that was to take many turns.

I often recall with some humour how, after successfully defending his title, Ali in February 1978 was defeated in Las Vegas by Leon Spinks. He took his defeat with his usual arrogance and bad grace and declared, "I will return," and so he did, to regain the world heavyweight title nine months later. However, commentators were convinced that on that fateful night in Las Vegas it was a watershed for the great man. Ali's boxing career was coming to an end. In 1981, now on medication for a crippling disease, the man who said "I am the greatest" was finished, never to return to the boxing arena.

When Ali said those famous words "I will return" he may not have realised that someone much greater had said it and will fulfil it. The gospel writer John records the words of Jesus, "I will come again and receive you unto myself." In the book of Acts, men in white robes say as Jesus leaves this earth, "This same Jesus will come again as you have seen him go." This is no ill-conceived comment, but an amazing promise.

Reflecting on the coming of Jesus, we rejoice in His first coming but also His coming again. It is the great hope of the Christian. As many of us struggle with the difficulties, suffering and temptations of this life, how tremendous are the words of St Paul in Romans chapter 8, "I consider that our present sufferings are not worth comparing with the glory that will be revealed in us."

While none of us knows the day or hour of Christ's return, the Bible strongly commends that we watch, wait and be ready for that day.

I am the greatest!

WHAT'S IN A NAME?

We were on holiday a few years ago when we met a lady from Scotland. Being in a hotel with strangers, I usually try to remember names, but I'm not always successful. Having asked the lady the second time to remind me of her name, she told me it was Amanda. Later, at the dinner table, she related to us the humorous background to her name. "I was the first born in the family and my parents were at odds as to what to call me. 'Why don't you call her after yourselves?' suggested the midwife, 'A Ma and Da, thus Amanda.'" The story raised a laugh around the table.

I suppose we all have stories about our names. My wife was expected to be born at Christmas. Her parents thought Carol would be appropriate if they had a girl, but she came thirty-two days later; nevertheless her parents stuck with their original choice. I have a close friend who calls himself Ken, but this was never allowed in the presence of his mother. She insisted he was called Kenneth, as in the Belfast parlance she maintained a Ken (can) was something men drank their tea out of in the shipyard.

Interestingly, in the Bible names have even greater significance. In the Old Testament God changed Abram's name to Abraham, to mean he would be the father of a multitude. Simon was renamed Peter by Jesus, meaning a rock. Saul's name was changed to Paul, perhaps a name more acceptable to the Gentiles.

One name, sadly, is often used blasphemously. And even religiously minded people are embarrassed using it. It is of course the name Jesus.

It has an all significant meaning. In the ancient Hebrew it was pronounced Yeshua. But whatever way we use it, it is the name God gave to His Son. The angel Gabriel revealed to Mary that they should "call his name Jesus, as He will save His people from their sins." And that's how significant His name is. St Peter preaching on the day of Pentecost revealed that all who call on this name can be saved. Throughout the centuries, millions have called on that name and been transformed and given hope in the midst of despair.

We must never use this name glibly or profanely. But as Peter assures us, if we use the name Jesus sincerely we can experience the forgiveness of our sins, the power to live a transformed life and a true hope for the life to come.

WHEN THE ICE MELTED

I will easily recall that February day. I was conducting the funeral of Beatrice who died at the ripe old age of eighty eight.

Making arrangements for her funeral, I was prompted to ask a family member if her niece Carol, who lives in London, would be present. They assured me she was. On the day it was snowing, freezing cold and miserable as a handful of people gathered at the Funeral Church.

When Carol arrived, I greeted her warmly and asked, "Would you like to say a few words of tribute to your auntie Beatrice?" She readily agreed. After a hymn and a prayer, she rose to speak. And this is what she said:

"Many years ago, my life was completely messed up, I was a druggy and an alcoholic drifting from place to place. My life was terrible. One day, remembering that the only Christian I knew

London City Mission

in the family was my auntie Beatrice, who lived on the Shankill Road, I made my way to her wee house. I was seeking help to turn my life around and that day Beatrice gave me a Bible. It had a broken zip and throughout her life she never stopped apologising for not giving me a better looking copy. In the days ahead I read that wee Bible and it led me to the point where I met with Jesus. My life has never been the same since."

The cold outside the Funeral Church seemed to melt into heat. At that moment on that drab winter day the gloom disappeared and I had a 'wow moment'!

But Carol's story doesn't end there. For many years now she has worked with the London City Mission, helping many who were once like her. Carol is now part of a Christian outreach café in the London Docklands. Every day she tells her story and shares this good news with anyone who is willing to listen.

For us, the experience of having a relationship with the living Lord can be as life changing and transforming as it was for Carol, even when it all started with Auntie Beatrice's tatty Bible with a broken zip.

GAME CHANGING MOMENTS!

Where I grew up there was only one sort of football, played with twenty two men and a round ball. As for rugby it was described as a hooligan's game played by gentlemen, while football was a gentleman's game played by hooligans. It was only in later years that I began to take an equal interest in both games. It is not surprising then that I spent a fair amount of time watching a recent Rugby World Cup. The obvious high profile of the game made the history of its origins for me somewhat fascinating. The apocryphal story of a young man called Webb Ellis at Rugby School, who in 1823 allegedly took up the ball and ran with it, first appeared in print in 1876, some four years after the death of a former Rugby schoolboy called Matthew Bloxam. Bloxam did not have first-hand knowledge of Webb Ellis, but quoted an unnamed person as his source of information on how the game started. Whatever the truth, this was a game-changing moment, as Webb Ellis is forever honoured and remembered with his name on the World Cup.

The fall of the Berlin Wall

Of course history is littered with moments that could be described as "game changing." As we stand in silence on Remembrance Sunday some of us reflect on what might have been, if the outcome had been a Nazi victory in World War Two. We thank God it didn't happen. In my lifetime the coming down of the Berlin Wall in November 1989 and the release of Nelson Mandela four months later were "game changing" moments. You may think of other such moments.

The Bible speaks of a time of expectation and waiting for the coming of the Messiah, to celebrate the moment in history when God put his foot on human soil in the person of the Lord Jesus Christ. It was to become, and continues to be, the greatest moment in history since creation. To refer to His coming as "game changing" is somewhat irreverent, but life-changing it truly is for the countless number who have received Him as their Saviour and Lord. They are now, as the gospel writer claims, the sons and daughters of God. They will not only share the history of His first coming, but will look for the wonder of His second advent when there will be a new heaven and a new earth: the greatest change of all, when He comes again in glory to reign forever.

William Ellis Statue

ALWAYS A MISSIONARY!

Kathie Cowan

Kathie Cowan was a fascinating woman. Born in 1916 in north Belfast it was at a missionary meeting that she heard about the awful conditions and problems women experienced in Japan and felt compelled to do something about it. In 1937 she went to the South Wales Bible College. Rather surprisingly it was there that she says she "really found Christ." She had a similar experience to that of Methodist founder John Wesley having previously "only a head knowledge of the gospel." Now her heart was "strangely warmed." During her time at college she fell seriously ill, and the staff thought that there was no possibility of her going anywhere in the world to serve God. Leaving college she trained as a nurse at St Bartholomew's Hospital in London (Barts), and eventually after a short time in Japan, she heard the call to South Korea. For sixteen years she served as a medical missionary with World Vision in a hospital supported by the American Presbyterian Church.

In South Korea, Kathie Cowan was responsible for leading many of the people under her care to a living faith in Jesus Christ. During her time there she was honoured by that government for outstanding public service. In her care were badly disabled children, some of whom had been written off by society. In the 1990s Kathie returned to South Korea on the invitation of the hospital in its centenary year, to be greeted by some of those she had helped. What a wonderful experience it was for her to find young people who had overcome their disabilities to serve Christ in an amazing way. Four of them were young men who had been rescued from begging on the streets; one who had disabilities in all four limbs was a now a pastor and had founded the Disabled Christian Fellowship of South Korea.

When Kathie returned to Northern Ireland she continued to be involved in Christian work. I first met her when she joined the East Belfast Mission congregation in the late 1980s. Eventually she helped in our Hostel for the Homeless and had a real understanding of the difficulties some of the homeless men and women were experiencing. She became their confidante and friend.

During my life Kathie was an inspiration, always encouraging and offering wise advice, and more than anything else, praying for me. One day in November 2003 she rang me, having not heard from me for a while. She said, "On Sunday 9th November a voice said to me, 'Go and pray for Jim Rea, he needs your prayers, he is in some difficulty.' At four o'clock that day Kathie went into her little room and prayed, not fully knowing the reason why. Kathie wanted to ring me immediately but couldn't, as she had completely lost her voice with laryngitis. On that Remembrance

Sunday in 2003 around lunchtime I was taken into the Craigavon Area Hospital with a heart attack. I recovered, and often think how that good woman was in touch with the Lord. How all of us need people like that in our lives! Kathie continued to encourage. She was always a missionary, right up until her death in her mid-nineties. No one who ever met Kathie Cowan will forget the experience.

Korean village

THE GIRL WHO SAID "THANKS" TO THE MAN WHO MADE A DIFFERENCE

I have known Sam for many years. He came to the East Belfast Mission having watched our morning service on television. What he did not know was that I knew him by reputation. In his early life he had been the ever popular youth club leader in Cregagh Methodist Church. Having worked there after Sam had moved on, I heard about his amazing Christian influence amongst the young people. I always longed to meet him. So when I met him that first Sunday I was keen to get to know him better. I soon discovered Sam's great talents. Not only was he an able administrator having a background in accountancy, but he had a great love for young people. When we opened a homework club on the Newtownards Road adjacent to East Belfast Mission to help motivate children and young people to develop and value education, Sam was a ready volunteer.

With his cloth cap and calm demeanour he was a hit. He knew every young person by name. He had a calming effect upon them, especially those who came from difficult family backgrounds. Time was no problem to this man of outstanding patience and generosity.

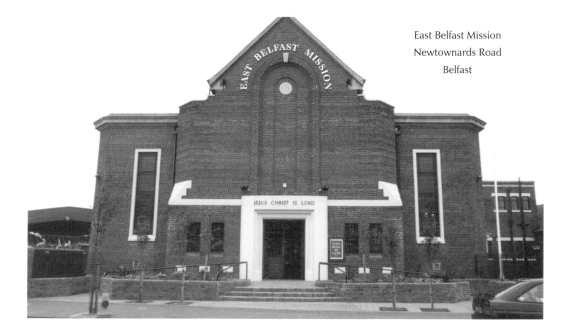

East Belfast Mission
Newtownards Road
Belfast

In his last days Sam was in a Nursing Home in Co Down. One day he shared with me that out of the blue an attractive young woman had come to see him. Initially he didn't have a clue who she was. Now a qualified accountant and working in a senior position in a Belfast business, she told Sam that what she had become in life, she owed to him. It soon clicked: it was Rhona, and he remembered her well – she had been a regular at the homework club. Now she said it with flowers and a box of chocolates. He was deeply moved by her expression of love and kindness.

As Sam told me the story, I thought, "Wasn't that nice of Rhona!" Very often we remember people affectionately but we never get around to saying thanks. It meant a lot to Sam. It made me think of the number of times thanks or thanksgiving is mentioned in the Bible. I think of Paul lying in prison in Rome thinking about his Christian friends at far way Philippi, so he writes to them: "I thank God every time I remember you." Another Bible reference about giving thanks comes from the Psalmist and is directed at the Lord Himself,

What can I offer the LORD
  for all he has done for me?
I will lift up the cup of salvation
  and praise the LORD's name
  for saving me.
I will keep my promises to the LORD
  in the presence of all his people.

Psalm 116 v 12-14   -   Isn't it good to say "thanks"

WHEN A G.P. WAS NOT P.C.

I still recall the day we met on the street for the first time in Enniskillen. He introduced himself with his characteristic broad smile. Arthur Williams had come to work with the Methodist Church as a pastoral assistant. He appeared extremely warm and friendly and was full of enthusiasm for the new challenge, but it was when I heard his story that I was deeply moved. Arthur, while still a young man, was a recovering alcoholic. Brought up in Coleraine with a good education, he became a very talented rugby player. It was in the celebrations after rugby matches and the downing of drink that he became addicted to alcohol. However hard he tried he was unable to stop. The future looked bleak.

Arthur Williams

Such was the extent of his alcoholism that he needed psychiatric support. One day in a moment of desperation he went to see his G.P., the highly respected Dr Bill Holley, at his practice on the Lodge Road in Coleraine. The doctor looked at Arthur and said, "Arthur, I can give you anti booze tablets if you want," and then made some remarks that may not be politically correct in today's world. "Arthur, Jesus Christ is risen, Jesus Christ is alive." He invited Arthur to pray. It was a defining moment that ultimately led to Arthur's deliverance from alcoholism to experience the transforming power of Jesus Christ.

One day visitors from Scotland attended Darling Street Methodist Church and happened to hear this dynamic young preacher. They went back to Glasgow to their church and there followed an invitation to Arthur to be pastor of Findlay Memorial Evangelical Church in inner city Glasgow. He soon realised that the area he worked in was full of people with addiction issues. He became burdened as to what he might do, and so he started group meetings and invited people with addiction issues to come. There was a remarkable response and it was a success. People openly shared their stories but always there was an emphasis on the God who could change lives.

Arthur made many discoveries. Not everyone overcame their addiction immediately. Some would relapse. Some would make it, some wouldn't, but God's patient love was always available and no one was beyond hope. Arthur put people around him who were free from their addiction and could inspire others towards a transformed life. As time went on Arthur Williams founded Stauros, a New Testament Greek word for cross. Today the Stauros Foundation works throughout the island of Ireland, the U.K. and the Isle of Man, offering the Christian hope that Jesus Christ is alive and can transform people's lives, just as Arthur found that day in the presence of Dr Bill Holley and, more important, the living Lord.

In the early 1980s I invited Arthur to speak to our congregation in east Belfast. He told the story of Stauros and with others we caught the vision too. Hence in 1985 the establishment of the East Belfast Mission, which saw central to its work, the reaching out to the many addicted people with a message of hope. That meeting with Arthur ten years before didn't happen by chance.

Arthur Williams called home 21st May 2019.

Coleraine town square

FERMANAGH'S LOST SON

Three days after our arrival in Irvinestown Co. Fermanagh in 1972 our doorbell rang. The caller was Arthur Moffitt. From that day on, without fully realising it at the time, I had a friend for life. Arthur Moffitt was an active local preacher in the Methodist Church, who grew up in Tierwinney Methodist Church near Ederney. He knew the area where I had been appointed to, intimately. He was to give me much advice as I

adjusted from being a city boy to working in a rural community. Over the next number of years I was learn much more about this remarkable man.

Talking modestly about his army career, he confessed that in 1943, much against the advice of a Godly mother, he joined the British Army. In fact he lied and forged his papers as he was 18 months underage. Describing himself as the "black sheep" who came from a devout Methodist upbringing, he was in the years following to experience the ravages of war. Assigned to the Royal Scots Guards, he recalled the invasion of France and landing in Normandy. He was wounded, but many of his comrades perished at his side. After rehabilitation he was stationed in India to help halt the threatened Japanese invasion into Burma. Now a Lance Corporal, he guarded the Japanese prisoners of war. His experience made him see war as a last resort. Violence should never be the way. The inhumanity of it all motivated him to treat the prisoners he was guarding with compassion. Eventually he was reassigned to the Middle East as a Military Policeman on a peace keeping mission between the Jews and Palestinians, before he was discharged.

Sunday the 1st September 1946 was the most significant day of his life. For whatever reason, he attended a Methodist service in the City of Bombay, now Mumbai. The preacher was a local Indian man who took for his subject the Prodigal Son. Arthur the soldier, now addicted to drink and tobacco, describes how he was confronted by the reality of Gospel. "The lost son was Arthur," he reflected on how his experience was mirrored in the Gospel story. He once wrote, "I received the kiss of forgiveness, the ring on my finger, and became adopted into the family of God." He was now in God's army and was to become, as St Paul describes it, "a good soldier of Jesus Christ."

Arthur has now in another Army's parlance, the Salvation Army, been "promoted to glory." I cherished his friendship.

Arthur Moffitt

Postscript: Arthur's niece Ruth was a young woman in her teenage years in the 1970s. She was very close to her uncle Arthur and very much influenced by him as he preached often in Tierwinney Methodist Church in rural Fermanagh. Sometimes along with a few dozen of a congregation she would hear some of my stories from the pulpit. One day in the early 2000s she was prompted to write me a letter with a gift telling me in the strongest terms that I must write a book. The thought never left me, but took many years to bring to fruition. I pray now that her encouragement has also made a difference.

GETTING OUT OF DEBT

I was brought up in a day when people got into debt. There were no credit cards or bank overdrafts available. People in working class Belfast communities lived from hand to mouth. The easy way to get a few shillings was via the pawnshop. The deal was you gave in an item of value, a watch, a ring, almost anything. The pawnbroker gave you something for it and handed you a ticket which allowed you to go back later to redeem the item or buy it back at a higher cost. The possibility of borrowing caused my mother to panic as she often lived hand to mouth.

How the world has changed! Debt is now far more sophisticated. We use words like liquidity or solvency, and refer to 'the credit crunch.' The amount countries owe as they speak of trillions is beyond the comprehension of most of us. Bail-outs for E.U. countries which are hard to mentally process are soon felt on the streets with job losses and closures happening every day.

Maybe the time is ripe to offer a different reflection on debt, to recognise that the Christian faith has something important to say about it. The Bible teaches us not to owe money in a way that we cannot repay it, to pay fair wages and to act justly. It urges us to flee from the love of money, to live in a spirit of contentment and to depend on God in life's most trying moments. But it also teaches something much more profound. There is a debt we can never repay. We cannot pay God back for our wrong doing. Jesus Christ shared our human nature, and on the cross represented us to God the Father. Forgiveness through an amazing act of grace is at the heart of the gospel.

I recall vividly as far back as the 1950s a neighbour woman showing me the wee buff coloured pawn ticket given to her by the pawnbroker. On it were words that lodged in my memory, it said 'to redeem.' I had seen them somewhere else. In the Bible! Joe Malcolmson our Sunday School teacher had explained what redemption really meant. 'To buy back.' He would remind us that in ancient times the term was used specifically in reference to the purchase of a slave's freedom. The application of this term to Christ's death on the cross is quite telling. If we are "redeemed" then our prior condition was one of slavery. God has purchased our freedom, and we are no longer in bondage to sin or to the Old Testament law. Redemption is at the centre of the Christian message. The Apostle Peter contrasts the value of material things with what Jesus has accomplished on the cross.

"For you know that it was not with perishable things such as silver or gold that you were redeemed from the empty way of life handed down to you from your ancestors, but with the precious blood of Christ, a lamb without blemish or defect." 1 Peter 1:18-19. Yet there remains our need to respond: Paul implores us to be reconciled to God. The 19th century Irish hymn writer Mrs Frances Cecil Alexander's words remain timeless:

He died that we might be forgiven,
He died to make us good,
That we might go at last to heaven,
Saved by His precious blood.

Geddis Pawn Shop Albertbridge Road Belfast

WHEN YOU CAN'T REVERSE

I once knew an elderly man who drove a car. My friend could never get it into reverse. The stories told about him were apocryphal. He was often seen parking his car in open spaces so that reversing would be unnecessary. Neighbours told me that he physically pulled the car backwards out of his driveway with a tow rope. His family consistently urged him to stop driving, but with little success.

Reversing is an interesting word and it's not just to do with driving. When I look at my holiday snaps of yesteryear I ask 'who's that fellow?' I smile for ageing is certainly irreversible. How often have we watched the despair of fans and players when that final penalty kick is missed in a cup final, the match is lost and the result will never be reversed.

But then what about the mistakes we have made? How often have we heard it said, "Looking back I should have known better." Not too many of us could sing with Frank Sinatra, "Regrets, I've had a few, but then again, too few to mention." For so many their lives are filled with them.

In the Bible there's a story of King David who messed up his life badly, and once wrote as a result of his failure, "My sin is ever before me." Peter wept bitterly when he realised he had denied Christ. St Paul never covers up his failures as he describes his role in the persecution of Christians and refers to himself as "the chief of sinners."

The past cannot be changed and the consequences of it often live on. Yet if you hold to the Christian viewpoint then the central theme of the cross of Jesus Christ is forgiveness. On the cross He took the shame and the blame for our sins.

For many, how they have lived or what has happened to them has radically changed their lives, often with horrendous consequences. Yet this word of hope remains. The repentant sinner will be forgiven and a new life will begin with Jesus Christ. That's why St Paul could say, "If anyone be in Christ they are a new creation; old things have passed away and all things have become new." When I recall my old friend who could not reverse his car, I become aware that in life neither can we reverse, but by God's grace in Christ we can know forgiveness and move on.

LOADS WE CARRY

Harvest Suppers are a feature of church life in rural Ireland. I must have been to hundreds of them and there's enough food to feed the five thousand. Recently I watched several ladies gingerly carrying the most wonderful eats into a church hall. One lady balanced trays as she tried to close the boot lid of the car and cling onto the sandwiches at the same time.

The incident reminded me of a story I heard some time ago about a woman who was driving her car. She was carrying a load of food to feed a couple of hundred people at a church event. Worried that some of it would get thrown about in the car, she was driving slowly and very carefully. This was much to the disgust of an irate motorist following behind. He kept pressing on the horn with great impatience. She remarked to her passenger, "If only he knew the load I'm carrying he might be a bit more patient."

I liked that story because it made me think of my own impatience. My wife Carol often humorously reminds me of the saying, "Patience is a virtue, possess it if you can, often found in woman, but seldom in a man."

But the point of the story that struck me is related to the remark, "If only he knew the load I'm carrying ……" for it contains a deeper truth. What load are we carrying? What burden preoccupies us? People who sometimes test our patience may well be carrying a problem we know nothing about. As a pastor, I have made judgments on people and have felt irritated at times by moods and attitudes. It is often long afterwards when I have realised what was going on in the person's life.

Perhaps I know because I too have been preoccupied at times by troubling experiences. I have learned the value of a trusted friend, but more than anything it's the experience of the writer of Psalm 55 that has proved helpful. The psalmist King David finds his life under threat. He is so deeply troubled that he contemplates escaping, running away, wandering afar heading for the wilderness. Suddenly, out of what is a grim read, comes this amazing word of enlightenment when he adds, "Cast your burden on the Lord, and He will sustain you." This truth has never failed me and I guess I speak for a multitude of others. If your load is hard to bear, take a quiet moment and throw, hurl, or give it over, to the Lord, for that's what the original word in the Hebrew language of Psalm 55 verse 22 really means.

Harvest Supper

LIVING OUT FAITH

A bus driver in New York became a Christian. He talked with a minister friend about how best he could live out his faith. He simply suggested that he see his bus as a 'Sanctuary.' The driver started greeting passengers with a smile and began helping disabled people who were waiting to board or leave his bus. After a number of months he reported back, saying with amazement how his approach had positively changed him and his passengers.

This story helped me recall the young lady who often sells me the morning newspaper. She smiles, asks about how I am and then makes an enquiry about someone I know who has health problems, whom she met briefly while herself in hospital. Then there is the medical receptionist who never seems to get flustered, she always smiles and gives me the information I require. I think of a friend who gives me money anonymously to pass on to people in need, and the postman who looks out for those on his delivery run and often buys food for a man begging on the street. I am aware that some of these I mention are Christians; however, the faith of others I do not know. What they have in common is their example of kindness and cheerfulness which impacts on me.

I am careful to point out that a relationship that brings us forgiveness and acceptance with God is not earned by good works or acts of charity. But should Christianity not be marked by such characteristics? The well-known Christian writer Dr. James Packer, when writing to people who had become Christians, reminds them that 'the only evidence of a past conversion is present convertedness'.

How often do we grump, groan, begrudge or sometimes show intolerance as we demean others whose politics, religion or culture are different to ours? No wonder we hear the saying that we have too much religion and not enough Christianity, with the added remark "They should practise what they preach." The example of that New York bus driver has made me think. He made his bus his sanctuary. The challenge for me is: wherever I find myself today and tomorrow, how with God's help can I do the same?

New York

ONLY CAME TO TAKE A PHOTOGRAPH!

The Colonel

As I held the baby the flash went on the camera for about the third time. "These people can be so insensitive," I thought. "You would think they would know better in a service of worship." However it wasn't uncommon for people to do strange things in this east Belfast church. "Who was that?" I tactfully enquired after the baptism. "Oh that was the baby's grandfather," I was told. I thought, "These amateur photographers are a right nuisance."

A few Sundays passed by, when I noticed the face in the congregation as I wrecked my brain on where I had seen him before. The penny dropped - it was none other than the cameraman, grandad himself. This time he was all alone with no baptismal party or fellow travellers. "Hello," I said as we shook hands at the end of the service. Then came the remark, "Could I have a word, reverend?" "No problem," said I, "if we can find a quiet space." With emotion in his voice he asked, "Would you say a prayer for me? I want to give my life over to the Lord and find his forgiveness." We prayed together, and I looked him up and down. "Guess you've been a soldier," I said, as I looked at the carefully bulled toecaps on the shoes. "Yes, Royal Ulster Rifles. I fought in Aden."

That encounter began a life changing experience for Jim who was to become a close friend to many of those who found life a struggle in that part of Belfast. His deportment soon gained him the nickname of "the Colonel."

The rest of his days were spent reaching out to those in greatest need. He soon became a familiar figure on the Newtownards Road. Down round the Mission you might see him playing a game of pool with a homeless man or looking for clothes or a bit of furniture for a needy person, or just offering a listening ear. No job was ever too difficult.

The Colonel died some years ago, but as I reflect on a life well lived and a man who had found real fulfilment through a living faith in Jesus Christ, I will always remember that first meeting and the flashes of the camera. I often joked with him about that first day, as we shared a bit of banter. When visitors from all parts of the world came to visit the Mission, they would often ask, "Jim, how do you come to be here?" With a twinkle in the eye he would look over at me and say, "Well I really only came to take a photograph."

REX FROM CASTLEWELLAN

I will never forget Rex. He was extremely friendly and delighted with our hospitality. I met him for the first time many years ago at Castlewellan Forest Caravan Park. There he was, grabbing my attention as he looked up at me and wagged his tail. I called him Rex and he seemed to respond. I couldn't quite work out what breed he was. At a guess I thought that his mother may have been a poodle and his father a springer spaniel, but despite his matted coat, he was a good looker. Rex was incredible, he begged for food, sat quietly and affectionately beside our caravan as he did with those on either side of us. He had no collar or ID and it was the opinion of the caravaners that Rex was a stray. Our neighbouring caravaners decided that he needed a home. At the end of the week he enthusiastically jumped into their car and they departed with their new addition. Our three children waved him a tearful goodbye. My wife Carol had put her foot down and said that there was no home for Rex in east Belfast.

A few days passed and then it happened: familiar faces appeared on the Caravan Park. It was our neighbours, who hastily pushed Rex out of their car. "What's wrong?" I asked. "What's wrong?" the woman replied sharply, "he barked the house down night and day and we couldn't stick it any longer." As Rex made his way into the nearby field, the family quickly departed. A few days later I noticed Rex receiving the hospitality of some other caravaners. At the same time I was talking to the ranger. I asked curiously, "Do you see that wee dog, do you know anything about him?" He laughed. "Oh," he said, "That dog lives in the housing estate in the town, he comes over here every year during the summer for his holidays." Looking at the colour of the flags in the estate I thought Rex might be green in his politics but in fairness he never showed a political bias as he gobbled up the caravaners' food.

The one thing I discovered was that in his doggy brain Rex knew where he really belonged, as he romped around under the Mountains of Mourne. More than for any wee dog, belonging is very important to all of us, whether it be nationality, identity, who we are, British, Irish Nationalist, Unionist, Republican. I often wonder if we really stop to think of the privilege and wonder of belonging to Jesus Christ. Discovering that means finding where we really belong. And it will remain when Ireland and "Norn Iron" are no more.

Here is how the Apostle Peter puts it:
> But you are a chosen people, a royal priesthood, a holy nation, a people belonging to God, that you may declare the praises of him who called you out of darkness into his wonderful light. 1 Peter 2 v 9

Castlewellan Rex

JOE MORRISON AND SIX CHURCHES

Fermanagh Lake

When I think about today's credit crunch and the banking industry, I remember the night I met Joe Morrison - a real character to say the least! Joe was a Cockney who had come to live in Northern Ireland after he married his wife, who preferred the freedom and the breezes of her home county in the Ulster Lakeland to the stifling lifestyle of London. Joe and his wife made the move to a caravan, in the garden of his mother-in-law's home.

Joe dabbled in all kinds of little cures for all kinds of diseases. His knowledge intrigued me, stimulating my interest in alternative medicine. I shared one of my remedies and he was mightily impressed; he thought that if he were to add some of his own extras to the remedy, we would stamp out the common cold worldwide and become millionaires. He said he would call it 'The Reamorr Cold Cure', putting the names of Rea and Morrison together. It mustn't have worked for I never reaped any financial benefits and nor did Joe.

Joe was a bit of a sceptic towards the church. Often he would share his own thoughts, or excuses, for non-attendance. While he admired its Founder, church wasn't for him. One frosty January evening in his caravan we chatted at length. As I looked around I could only think of the Belfast woman who rang the Housing Executive and in her words complained that the "condescension was running down her walls" for damp was everywhere in Joe's caravan. As he rolled another cigarette he claimed, "There are six churches in this town." I only knew of four so I was up for an argument. He insisted that there were six. Pointing the finger he said, "There is the Northern Bank and the Ulster Bank - they are churches too you know. If I read it right, a lot of people around here, that's where they worship." I reflected for a moment. "You might be right, Joe," I replied.

After a cup of tea I made my way into the cold of the night. I realised that was how some people had impacted on this stranger. I knew many in the town who weren't like that at all. Nevertheless these words of Jesus came to mind, "No servant can serve two masters. Either he will hate the one and love the other, or he will be devoted to the one and despise the other. You cannot serve both God and Money."

Ulster Bank Waring Street Belfast

WHAT TIME IS IT?

When the end of October comes I experience a slight degree of negativity. The great celebrations of the harvest services have come to an end, and on the last Sunday in the early hours, it will happen: we will put the clock back and return to the dark days of the approaching winter. Oh dear, short days don't really do with me!

A humorous story from well over forty years ago always comes to mind. James Hetherington was a retired farmer and a member of the church I served in Irvinestown. One afternoon I recall sitting with him in his kitchen. I noticed his clock was an hour fast. "Five o'clock, James, surely it's only four!" With a smile he replied, "I keep it at summertime all year round, it makes me feel better." Momentarily I experienced a degree of empathy on that dark winter day.

I had to admire James' laid-back approach, a contrast to today when we live by the clock and possess time pieces that claim accuracy to within seconds.

Clocks weren't invented in Bible times, but nevertheless the scriptures have a lot to say about time. The 90th Psalm, attributed to Moses and probably written over three thousand years ago, remains relevant when it states that the life expectancy of a person is around seventy years, but perhaps in some cases with extra strength, eighty years. The author of Ecclesiastes writes poetically about the subject, saying that there is a time for everything and a season for every activity under the sun. St Peter is even more profound, stating that with the Lord a thousand years are as a day, and a day as a thousand years.

Time is above all a gift from God that many of us take for granted. Walter Payton was one of the greatest ever American footballers. He died in 1999 aged forty-five. His words are much more famous than his name, because it was he who said, "Tomorrow is promised to no one."

An old Belfast character I knew, when asked "Please mister, what time is it?" would look at his watch and kindly oblige, but then would graciously add, "It is also time to seek the Lord" - words from the book of Hosea. A timely thought!

Harvest at Scrabo

AN UNPLEASANT WORD

I seem to recall that, when attempting to purchase an item over the internet, I received a polite reminder that my MasterCard had expired. I should have known, because when I look at my card I see the words 'valid from' followed by 'expires end'. Of course the word expired is used in different ways, as is 'best before' which some of us may at times have ignored. I am reminded of the funny story of the lady who rang a turkey provider to ask if the turkey in her freezer for the last six years would be edible. She was assured that it would be ok but was likely to be tasteless, to which she responded, "Oh that's ok, I will give it to the church."

I do recall hearing that someone had expired, meaning they had died. It is a word seldom used these days to refer to a person's death, but in another age someone who had died would have been said to have expired. The famous 19th century actor Joseph Jefferson once remarked, "We are only tenants, and shortly the great Landlord will give us notice that our lease has expired." Look around old churchyards and you may well find the words on some of the gravestones.

While we know that the credit card and the food warning provide us with a date, what we don't know is when our final expiry date will be.

Rightly St Paul describes death as the last enemy to be defeated. None of us can underestimate the trauma of loss, or the experience of grief. Jesus Himself wept at the death of Lazarus.

Healing and adjustment take time after we lose someone we love. Glib words such as "time heals" or "she is in a better place" can rightly be perceived as trite. Yet death is the inevitable outcome for all of us. We cannot last forever in this present state. St Paul speaks of our body being a temporary structure, a tent.

On the other hand the Bible doesn't want us to be pessimists but rather to be eternal optimists. It promises life in heaven forever to the person who puts their trust in Christ. Much better than anything we have experienced in this life! No day is too late or indeed too soon to begin this journey to a life that never expires.

Words from the song Amazing Grace say it all:

When we've been there ten thousand years,   *We've no less days to sing God's praise*
Bright shining as the sun,   *Than when we'd first begun.*

Joseph Jefferson - "We are only tenants"

L.B.W. FOR THE WRONG REASON!

On a summer Saturday afternoon I'm usually to be found on the boundary at a local cricket ground. A local cricket match is a great place to spend an afternoon for those who can. It's not only the game but the stories one hears from those sitting around the boundary. One story in particular always draws a laugh.

In bygone days there was a well-known cricket umpire, we'll call him Tommy. He travelled all over the rural parts of Northern Ireland to games. However, he had a particular problem: he always needed to use public transport, in those days it was UlsterBus, which meant that wherever he was, he needed to catch the bus back to Belfast. From rural villages and towns the last bus was around 7.30 or 8.00pm. The story goes that if a team won the toss, the message from the captain was, "bat first," for with Tommy's bus home in mind, it would be said that every appeal against the team batting in the second innings would be given. Especially if it was L.B.W., then immediately Tommy's finger would go up, and the batsman would be out. The prevailing issue was Tommy's bus home, not the rightness of the decision! The story, while creating loud laughter, has nevertheless serious implications. It was judgement given with an ulterior motive. Albeit it was only a cricket match.

All of us inevitably make wrong decisions and with hind-sight politicians occasionally admit to them, while judges seldom do. Unfortunately football referees often have their decisions scrutinised and criticised under TV replay. Truthfully in whatever walk of life we find ourselves, looking back at judgements we have made, we have so often got it wrong.

What is of course much more reprehensible is the decision given for a selfish reason. On that one, umpire Tommy must be pronounced guilty. Natural moral justice causes us to recoil, when we hear a decision obviously made with a hidden motive. Sadly in this community, dominated by sectarianism and leaving us with countless victims, the cry for justice often seems to go unheard and accounts for the often one-word outburst "WHY?"

Getting it wrong is one thing, but deliberately not doing what is right is a different matter. Protecting self-interest at the cost of another is at very heart of human nature. The Bible refers to it starkly with one word, "sin." It is that bias in each of us towards self-centredness. The Bible teaches that God the judge of the entire world has the final say and will ultimately do what is right. Yet balanced with that judgement is His mercy, gained for us when Christ took our sins to the cross and made forgiveness possible. However, that is only validated when we repent of our sins, and indeed show the good works that follow true repentance. In this community when we hear the indefensible defended to protect self-interest, there's a bigger lesson in the story of Tommy than simply his need to catch the bus.

IT'S WHAT HE SEES!

Ian Botham with Jonathan Rea

As a TV sports watcher I often think to myself, who would referee or umpire these days as TV pundits pore over slow motion replays, which they examine from every angle? "Was he out, yes?" says one, as the other remarks, "I'm not sure, let's look at it again." The mounting pressure of the TV camera has brought video technology into several sports to make the final decision. And so we experience the tension of the rugby referee with hand over the ear piece going up top and asking, "Was it a try?" Or we watch the big screen in the cricket ground that seems to take ages to show - OUT! or NOT OUT!

I asked a cricket umpire one day, tongue in cheek, "Davy, do you ever get it wrong?" He paused, smiled and then replied, "Yes of course I do. But then you know it's not what you see, it's what I see." His answer sent my mind in another direction as I recalled a picture which hung on a bedroom wall. It said, "Thou, Lord, seest all things." In my youth I found it disturbing and it probably underpinned my earlier experience of a mother who reminded me constantly that when I misbehaved, God was looking down at me.

Later in life I have actually found the thought helpful as I have listened to the hurts of people who felt they had been the victims of evildoers, or had experienced terrible misjudgements or wrong decisions which had deeply affected their lives.

Of course, God seeing all things may well provide cold comfort if you are the victim. Interestingly the story of Joseph, one who was a victim, is told in the book of Genesis. He was a man wronged by his brothers and later falsely accused by his master's wife, leading to a prison sentence - but in the end God vindicated him and the dreadful experience worked out for good, as he became the minister for agriculture in the government of Egypt. He was able eventually to say, "They meant it to harm me but God meant it for good." The Bible assures us that God does see all things and that He, the judge of all humanity, will put things right, if not in this life, certainly in the life to come.

What my umpire friend said on that sunny afternoon many years ago as we watched cricket on the boundary, did make me think. It's true it's not what we see, but what He sees.

It's what he sees

WHAT CAN I GIVE BACK?

"We have become a culture of grumblers," a friend said to me recently. Certainly when I listen to the radio phone-ins, complaints from listeners seem to dominate the airwaves. The politicians, the health chiefs, the electricity providers and a plethora of others come under constant fire. It made me recall a quote I read recently, which said, "If you can read you are better off than two billion people, who are unable to do so. If you can attend a church without fear of harassment, or worse, then you are better off than three billion people in the world. If you have food in the fridge, clothes on your back, a roof over your head and a place to sleep, then you are richer than three-quarters of your fellow beings."

I then thought of the day I took a friend Chris and his family from Iowa on a visit to the Belfast City Hall. They were highly impressed by the great building and the wonderfully animated guide, who explained in detail the amazing social history of Belfast. She pointed to the Latin motto for the city, "Pro tanto quid retribuamus," informing us that it was from Psalm 116 verse 12, which asks the question "What shall I render unto the Lord for all his benefits toward me?" My American friend remarked, "What a good motto." "I wish we took it more seriously," I added cynically.

The motto is of course a reminder that a thankful spirit and a personal trust in God were central to the Christian faith espoused by the early founders of Belfast, who desired to give something back to the Lord in return. Perhaps at times their motto didn't always reflect their actions, any more than it appears to reflect the attitudes of so many today. But we take note of the Belfast motto, not just by a visit to the City Hall, but to practise it in how we treat others. Saying thanks to the Lord involves generosity and love towards our neighbour whoever they may be. Now just in case you get it wrong: not for one moment am I suggesting we shouldn't hold people to account. I'm all for that. But we might consider asking ourselves, "What shall I render to the Lord for all his benefits to me?"

Belfast City Hall

WHAT WOULD JESUS DO?

An old friend of mine is always good for a story. He tells one about the Sunday School class in which the teacher instructed the children that if they ever faced a difficult decision they should ask themselves the question, "What would Jesus do?" One day for whatever reason a discussion arose. If they were on their way to the cinema with two shillings for the entrance fee, only to discover a very sick man begging on the pavement, what would they do? After some time for thought, the teacher asked, "Now what would Jesus do?" One little boy immediately replied, "Miss, He would heal the man and go on to the pictures." Now you might know I will never defend the authenticity of this story in court, but the little boy's reply was brilliant, if not profound.

Princess Cinema Newtownards Road

Recently I thought of this story as I made my regular drive up by the Shankill/Falls peace line. I am always intrigued by the tourists signing their names on the wall.

Mural at Newtownards Road Belfast

96

Most days as I drive around Belfast, images stare me in the face. Some of them in fairness display excellent artwork portraying our history, in some cases remembering the lives of people lost in our troubled past. But then there are images of gunmen looking down at me in a threatening manner and on many occasions I observe hate filled slogans. My heart sinks! And then the question comes back, "What would Jesus

Graffiti on Belfast Peace Wall

do?" about these walls and slogans. I wonder would He bring in a demolition squad to deal with the walls and a team of painters to cover the graffiti?

Perhaps not! On the contrary, if we would only let Jesus heal the walls of division in our hearts, transform our attitudes, set us free from the old hatreds that still linger and set us new priorities to love Him and our neighbours as ourselves, we might be truly surprised what would happen.

For
where there is hatred, we would sow love;
where there is injury, pardon;
where there is doubt, faith;
where there is despair, hope;
where there is darkness, light;
and where there is sadness, joy.

So that wee boy's answer in the Sunday School class still keeps coming back to me in so many ways, even though I can just about remember when two shillings got you into the cinema.

THE ETERNAL TRANSPLANT

Freeman Hospital Newcastle

May was a feisty wee Shankill Road woman. A great character, she was dogged with ill health, and was dependent on twenty four hour oxygen support. From time to time she would be called to the Freeman Hospital in Newcastle upon Tyne, to be assessed for a lung and heart transplant. Through all of this she showed incredible courage despite increasing weakness. She was full of humour, quick witted, and always had an answer for you. Over several years she spent much time in hospital, returning home for short periods.

One day visiting her in her home, she seemed unusually subdued. Believing that there was every reason that she might feel depressed, I enquired how she was feeling. "Not good," she replied. And then came the surprising remark, "I am sitting here thinking, and I'm really sad. Somebody has to die so that I might live." It was a salutary moment. There was silence; I paused and then went into the preacher mode, "May, someone has died that you might live forever." She stared at me, then smiled, "That's the Lord you are talking about, I know that and I believe that." I knew then she had grasped the reality of the Easter message, the belief about the death and resurrection of Jesus Christ that by the grace of God it is possible to be forgiven and receive the hope of life forever.

It was a Maundy Thursday and I thought I would call to see May in hospital. Knowing that she wasn't a terribly religious woman and mightn't want to be quoted in church, gingerly I asked, "May, tonight in church I would like to tell a story about a woman needing a transplant, who believes that whatever the future holds, by trusting the Lord she has the better hope of life that lasts forever. But I won't use her name." Removing her oxygen mask, she said, loudly as only this Shankill Road woman could, "Oh by all means use my name, tell them who it is!" I did, and the congregation was deeply moved. Just a short time later May discovered the reality of this new life that lasts forever, and I was able to tell this story at her funeral service.

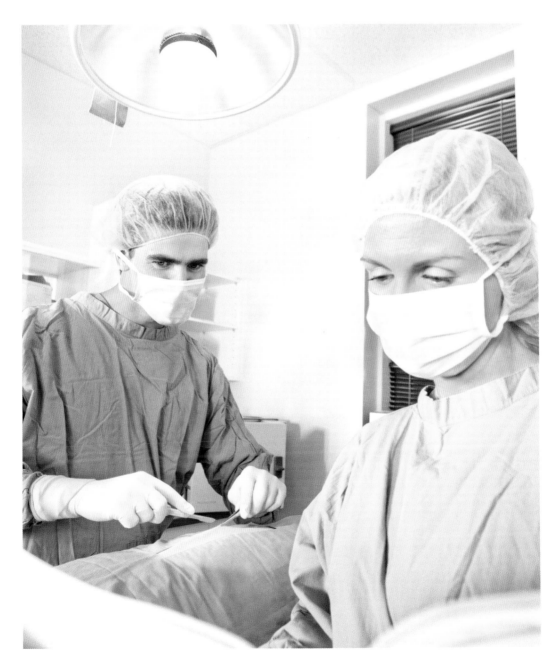

PLUGS IN YOUR EARS!

As I write, I hold my hands up and admit. I do not possess an iPhone or a smart phone. All I have is a very basic mobile. When I remove it from my pocket my friends often have a bit of a laugh. But unlimited calls and unlimited texts for nine pounds a month is hard to beat.

Believe it or not I do like gadgets, and I have several including an iPad. So let me explain. A few years ago I was travelling on the train from Coleraine. Four students from the University got on and sat down together. Immediately they put their earphones into their ears and began to swipe their screens. Throughout the journey, not a word was spoken. Suddenly a thought flashed into my mind: don't get one of those phones or you'll become addicted.

My rather old fashioned idea was confirmed some time later when we holidayed in Dublin. Being uncertain about getting on the right bus to our hotel, I sought the help of a Chinese lady. She told us she too was boarding our bus and that she would keep us right. As we got on she decided to sit beside us and we started to talk. And of course, nosey me asked her a few questions. She told us she had a responsible accountancy job in Dublin.

But then she admitted that she struggled with being away from home, and there was the unfamiliar Irish food, and of course the cost of accommodation. But she spoke warmly of the friendliness of Irish people and the variety and beauty of such a small country. She then asked me what I worked at. I told her I was minister.

"A pastor!" she exclaimed. She lit up. "I am a Christian too." She then told us about the evangelical church she attended in Dublin. She shared the difficulties for Christians in China, and how some Christians had to go underground, often meeting in forests and under trees. She acknowledged that despite its secularism there was freedom to be a Christian in Ireland. Unlike so many she spoke of her faith openly. As we left the bus the twenty minute conversation was for me and my wife Carol an inspiration. Statistics tell me that in China only one in around three hundred people claim allegiance to Christianity. Yet in my pocket today is a New Testament printed, would you believe, in China? God promises never to leave Himself without a witness and we had met one. As we left the bus, white plugs adorned the majority of ears. It was for me another blow to earphones and mobiles that have become conversation stoppers.

Great Wall of China

THE SAT NAV OFFERS A LESSON

Gordon Linney

Gordon Linney, the former Church of Ireland Archdeacon of Dublin, writes a stimulating weekly religious column in the Irish Times. Some time ago he wrote an article that struck a chord with me: the story of a young man who drove a long distance to attend a funeral.

On arrival at the funeral he had a conversation with an older man who was struggling with the circumstances of the death, causing him to remark, "You would wonder if there really is a Man above." The younger man immediately replied that in fact he had made the long journey to the funeral with the help of a woman from above. A surprising response you might say! Well, he was of course referring to his sat nav, an amazing device that was invented in its primitive form by a Japanese inventor as far back as 1961. Initially only used in military operations, it is now in a more sophisticated form found in almost every modern car. So just type in the postcode and the lady from above will get you right to your destination.

However, the point the young man may have wanted to make is even more profound. Perhaps he was suggesting how ridiculous it would have seemed to an earlier generation, that typing an address into a small screen would trigger a voice that would guide you to your destination. Our grannies and grandads would have accused us of experiencing hallucinations or just being completely off the wall.

However, if modern science does such unbelievable things, is it not just possible that there is someone who listens, guides, and watches over us?

Eugene Peterson the American theologian and poet, who has paraphrased the Bible into a modern idiom, takes a verse from the Book of Proverbs and puts it this way:

> *Trust God from the bottom of your heart;*
> *don't try to figure out everything on your own.*
> *Listen for God's voice in everything you do, everywhere you go;*
> *he's the one who will keep you on track.*
> (Proverbs 3:5-6)

An inspiring thought about a living and active God who is more anxious to guide us that we might ever imagine, who can keep us on track in a much more profound way than any sat nav with all its wonders.

Eugene Peterson

WHEN MINUS BECOMES PLUS!

I had just bought my spanking new little CD player. I put the batteries in, turned it on and nothing happened. Irate, I was almost back into my car to return it to the shop, when I paused for a moment. I must just check. Yes, I had done it again for the umpteenth time. I'd put the batteries in the wrong way round. I am sure there are more than a few readers who understand the problem. I have no knowledge of the science behind it all, but I should know minus stands for negative, while plus stands for positive.

These symbols of course have wide ranging connotations. In a different way I have experienced them throughout life. The difficulty of conducting a sad funeral in the morning, to the contrast of joining a happy couple together in marriage in the afternoon. Moving from a minus to a plus. It's a reminder that all of us oscillate between them both: life is full of both joys and sorrows, or as we say, "ups and downs." Some things are never simple or easily explained. There are the horrors of the displaced and the persecuted people of the world, the suffering and the hunger. On the same day that I watched on TV the appalling violence inflicted by Isis, this news is followed by the celebrations of supporters of the winning team after a Rugby international.

When reflecting on these opposites I recalled a piece of art work I saw some years ago. It was essentially an optical illusion. The negative sign, the minus, was clear to be seen, but contemplating it for a moment something became obvious. There was a less obtrusive vertical bar harder to see, but it changed the minus to a plus. It was of course the artist making a point.

It was the cross of Christ which turned the minus to the plus! What Jesus did on that cross has changed history. He took the punishment for our sins, whatever they are or however awful they may seem. An act of repentance on our part means we can be forgiven and have the sure and confident hope of a better life to come.

While evils of the world continue and questions remain about the suffering, the grief and the struggles of this life, the promise is that the events of Good Friday and Easter Day mean that whatever our experiences in life are, the message of the death and resurrection of Jesus ultimately turned negative to positive and minus to plus.

A ONE WAY STREET WITH A GATE

Rev Dr S Wesley Blair

"In whatever state I find myself, therein I am content." Words easier said than done. Written to Christians in Philippi by St Paul while imprisoned in Rome, they are often quoted in Christian circles, but sometimes sound glib. In contrast, they were quoted to me by a close friend after being told that he had possibly only weeks to live. "Read that verse to me," he insisted, and as I lifted a Bible to read, "this is where I am at," he exclaimed confidently.

Wesley was a Methodist minister, an outstanding academic, having achieved several degrees with a PhD from Queen's University, developing the relationship between physics and theology. He had a particular interest in the works of the famous 20th century theologian Karl Barth. Yet for all that, he told me that what was important to him was not the letters that appeared after his name, but the fact that he was first and foremost a preacher of the gospel. In the early 80s he left the field of science, to enter the ministry. Only months into his first appointment to a church in his mid-thirties, he was diagnosed with cancer, with a prognosis that looked grim, but he recovered. For over thirty years he had a multiplicity of recurring cancers and in 2011 he almost died from a cardiac arrest.

Wesley would often recount the story of Karl Barth who, being asked by a student to sum up in a sentence his life's work, replied "In the words of a song I learned at my mother's knee: 'Jesus loves me, this I know, for the Bible tells me so.'" He affirmed Barth's saying that every Christian preacher should read the newspaper and the Bible, but should interpret the newspaper from the Bible.

In Wesley's last weeks, he asked me for a copy of an old hymn containing these words, "Oh the love that drew salvation's plan, oh the grace that brought it down to man, oh the mighty gulf that God did span at Calvary." It is my lasting memory of a believer who knew what it meant to fully trust Jesus Christ. "I am on a one way street now," he said to me a few weeks before his passing. It was a one way street, but it had a gate that led him into the presence of his Lord forever. That really made a difference!

Queens University Belfast

WHO OWNS SAINT PATRICK?

It was the eve of St Patrick's Day and I was in Philadelphia taking a church service. Shaking hands with the congregation as they left the church, an American lady grinned from ear to ear as she shook my hand, "You know I'm Irish too," she said. The next day on a visit to a nearby mall I saw it all - everywhere was green! "Have a green pancake," said Wayne my pastor friend. "St Patrick's Day is big around here."

I was reluctant to tell him that in the streets of North Belfast where I grew up, we hardly knew of the Saint's existence. A bit extreme maybe, but for most of us St Patrick was a Catholic and belonged to the other side of the house, maybe even green in his politics . Mind you I did recall seeing his name on an Orange banner and on a few churches that took his name, but that was about the height of it. In "Norn Ireland" he still didn't warrant a national holiday.

I did go on to explain to my friend as we poured on the green syrup that sadly, where I grew up, if the ancient Saint was claimed by one side he would be fairly much ignored by the other. Now almost forty years on from that day, while things have improved, not everybody feels they can celebrate the great man. Maybe there is one thing I can chance saying about him: that if he was anything he certainly was truly a loyalist.

Now before you stop reading, let me explain. What is obvious is not his loyalty to a political ideal or religion, but his loyalty to Jesus Christ.

So who owns St Patrick? Well in a sense all of us on this island do. However, to own the Lord of St Patrick is of much greater importance than simply celebrating our cultural or political identity, good and worthy as that may be. He would mourn our division and inspire us to a Christ-centred faith that is over and above all forms of sectarianism or even religion, firmly rooted in the ultimate Kingdom of God.

I still see that lovely lady who said "I'm Irish too." I agree, and so am I, but to belong to the One whom St Patrick served can unite us all to a greater loyalty. In the sentiments of the ancient Saint may Christ be in the hearts of both friend and stranger. When it comes around, have a great St Patrick's Day.

"THERE BUT FOR THE GRACE OF GOD..."

Smithfield Market Belfast in the 50s

As brighter days come on after winter I often think of my old mate John (not his real name). In the late 1950s we attended Everton Secondary School in North Belfast. We had one thing in common, both of us disliked school. We were undisciplined and not good pupils. John came from the Hammer District of the Shankill. He was always sent to school well turned out. However if there was bit of skulduggery to get up to, John and I would be involved. As the summer approached and we would see the sun shining, we would go into school, get marked on the roll and then at break time, escape out the back gate and make our way to the old St Mary's cricket ground (now part of the Glencairn Estate) where we would lie in the sun and smoke a cigarette.

After I left school I lost touch with John but heard that he had joined the British Army. I was rather pleased, thinking that army life would be a good discipline for him, although I didn't think it was such a good idea for me. In the year before I left school something significant had happened to me, I got converted to Christ at a local Pentecostal Church. I was still a bit of a rascal but it gave me a different perspective to my life.

A few years passed and I was exploring the second hand bookshops and record stalls of the old Belfast Smithfield Market, when I was approached by a shadowy character who asked me for few shillings to get something to eat. It was my old friend John; we instantly recognised each other. He talked for a little while and told me that he had been given a dishonourable discharge from the British Army and

Shankill Road Belfast

was living rough. I felt very sad. I obliged him with some money, but with the thought that it might go on drink.

Some years later I was a student for the ministry and got invited to a Christian meeting in a house in North Belfast. After the meeting was over the lady of the house pressed a £5 note into my hand. It was a fortune in those days and a great help to a student minister. She was a lovely woman. She said, "Jim, will you pray for our John." It took a moment but then the penny dropped. This was John's mother. She gave me an address in the city where he lived and I looked him up. He was living in pretty bad conditions and I am not sure he really wanted to see me.

When the summer suns come out and I reflect on yesteryear, I still pray for my friend. I would love to meet him again. A friend of mine used to say when he looked at people whose lives were messed up, "There but for the grace of God go I." That saying always grips me, I am no better or less vulnerable than John who had a good upbringing and a Christian mother who loved him unconditionally. I always pray that he has found the God whose grace is unconditional. For didn't Jesus tell a story about a man who did come home and once again rejoiced?

TWO HARD HATS IN THE WARDROBE

I got to know Cyril though our work at the East Belfast Mission. Cyril had been introduced to me by Tommy who had overcome alcohol addiction and was sharing his new found faith with fellow sufferers. His influence had brought in Cyril, and soon he came to a living faith in Jesus Christ. Cyril had serious problems with alcohol and had been in several rehabilitation centres. Now he was part of the Mission congregation where he got great support. He was truly a new man in Christ. Having been an ex-Navy man he was always well turned out, and looked distinctive with his handlebar moustache. Added to his many attributes was his great sense of humour. He talked about his old days in the Navy and his introduction to drink. Some of the experiences of being a seaman were hilarious. He had also been an Orangeman and member of Whitewell Temperance L.O.L. He would laugh and say, "Temperance, that was some joke."

Never married and now in his early sixties, a lady in the congregation took a shine to him and invited him home on several occasions for tea. He boasted about her baking, her lovely home and the best china she put out for him. So you can guess he had to overcome some banter. "When's the big day Cyril?" we would ask, to which he would quickly retort, "No chance, there are two hard hats in the wardrobe!" He was referring to the fact that two husbands had predeceased this good lady and he didn't want to be the third. We would burst into fits of laughter.

It always reminds me that often we treat very serious things with humour. I never cease to be amazed, when visiting a home where there has been a recent bereavement, that there's always some wag making people laugh or telling funny stories about the deceased. When I asked a minister friend from Sierra Leone how his people had overcome some terrible atrocities in his homeland, he replied, "With a strong Christian faith and a sense of humour." We all know that laughter is great medicine.

The Bible is so profound on how it advises on life's most serious matters. It doesn't instruct us to be dull and gloomy or living with a constant death wish, nor on the other hand does it want us to neglect the importance of readiness for the life to come. How well it is all summed up in the words of the book of Proverbs 14:13: "Even in laughter the heart may ache, and rejoicing may end in grief."

DOOR OPENERS

The advice of the police is being taken more seriously these days, when they suggest caution about opening our doors to strangers. The message is certainly catching. As I go visiting, I am constantly confronted with stickers on doors with the words, "No cold callers!" Looking back to the 1970s when we lived in Fermanagh, I was amazed that nobody ever knocked a door but simply shouted "hello" and walked on in. Douglas and Kathleen Hudson's door was ever open in more ways than one. To my surprise they didn't even lock up when going to bed. It was a new experience to get that kind of welcome with the open door.

As I reflect on this I am also thankful for those who have opened doors for me in other ways. I can think of Ian and Eira who opened their door, fed and watered me for many weeks when I was student minister on a placement in Manchester. And there are Wayne, Bob and Chris who introduced me to America. Bettie and Ray who when we went to New Jersey U.S.A. in the 1980s opened their door, and made us feel we had known them for a lifetime. Today you might want to give thanks for someone who opened the door for you.

And then there's my friend Molly, a 94 year old lady that I would visit on the Shankill Road. She doesn't like cold callers. So it takes a few pushes on the doorbell before she opens somewhat abruptly. "Come on in!" she says loudly. Inevitably as I am about to leave with her complimentary packet of mints, she points, "That's my favourite!" Not the mints! It is a picture, not the 1850s masterpiece but a print of Holman Hunt's famous painting 'Light of the World.' It shows Jesus knocking at a long unopened door and is based on Revelation 3 v 20: "Behold I stand at the door and knock; if anyone hears my voice and opens the door, I will come in and eat with him and he with me." The door in the painting has no handle and can only be opened from the inside.

Today as I give thanks for my door openers, I am above all overwhelmed by the love of Jesus Christ who opens a door to salvation and eternal life to anyone who hears His knock and opens the door of their life to Him.

A HUG FOR TONY

Some years ago I heard a famous American preacher and raconteur speak at a prayer breakfast at the Stormont Hotel in Belfast. People from different political parties, Unionists and Nationalists, they were all there. Tony Campolo told how he was walking on Chestnut Street in North Philadelphia when he noticed a homeless man who looked filthy, smelt badly and had a beard full of rotten food. He was holding a cup of coffee. "Hey mister," he said to Tony, "do you want a sip of my coffee? It is McDonald's best. I think if God gives you something good you should share it."

Campolo thought he was being conned for a few bucks, so he asked, "Is there something I can do for you?" Expecting a request for money which he was ready for, he was shocked when the tramp exclaimed, "Yeah, you can just give me a hug." The tramp put his arms around Tony and held on to him, much to his embarrassment as people looked on. However, the preacher's feelings soon turned to awe as he heard a voice saying, "I was hungry; did you feed Me? I was naked; did you clothe Me? I was sick; did you care for me? I was the tramp you met on Chestnut Street; did you hug Me? For if you did…you did it for Me." The day Tony told the story at Stormont Hotel he added "That day I thought I was hugging Jesus Christ." As I looked around, political opponents were reduced to tears and the story was indelibly lodged in my memory. I will never forget it. It offers a remarkable lesson.

Chestnut Street Philadelphia

MISSING THE MAIN EVENT

Those of us who have visited the USA will often hear from the older people of some of the great hardships that came to the American people during the time of the Great Depression in the 1930s. I recall hearing a story told of a family who struggled to put food on their table. There was nothing to spare and they had no money for luxuries. So this story becomes relevant.

A circus was coming to town, when a youngster who had never seen a circus before, worked feverishly and eventually was able to buy a ticket.

On the day the circus arrived, he went to see the performers and the animals parade through town. As he watched, a clown came dancing over to him, and the boy, thinking it the right thing to do, put his ticket in the clown's hand. Then he stood on the kerb and cheered as the rest of the parade moved by.

The youngster rushed home to tell his parents what he had seen and how exciting the circus was. His father listened, then took his son in his arms and said, "Son, you didn't see the circus. All you saw was the parade." What a disappointment!

As I reflect on that story I often think of the disappointment and innocence of the little boy, and yet it is a parable that relates to the Christian faith. In Northern Ireland in particular, we sometimes get waylaid with so many other issues and distractions that we get our priorities wrong and miss the real thing.

How do we relate to Jesus Christ, who defeated death on the cross and makes eternal life a reality? That's the main event! Just like the wee boy, we could easily get sidetracked and miss it.

The circus comes to town

New York Stock Exchange

NO REVENGE

It was a summer day in the apple county of Armagh, and I was relaxing over a cup of tea with my friend Stephen, when he told me an amazing story about his late father.

I had met his father Eric when he was in declining health, but the story that unfolded moved me deeply. Stephen explained that for almost all of World War 2, having been captured by the Nazis, his father was consigned to a camp in Poland. Every day he would recall memory verses from scripture and pray, but he would at times question his faith and ask, "Lord, why am I here?"

During the day he was assigned to work on a farm, with the instructions that any contact with the farm owners would bring instant death before a firing squad. A period of time passed. One day a dispatch rider appeared on the farm lane and soon he heard a commotion in the farm house. The news was that Hans, a son of the farm owners, had been killed in action, fighting for the Nazis. His compassion compelled him to take a serious risk and go and knock the farmhouse door to offer his sympathy on the loss of their son. Despite great personal risks the farm owners were so moved that they began to secretly provide him with food and friendship.

One day things were to change dramatically: Eric heard loud gunfire, and suddenly a group of Russian soldiers stormed into the farm. The family with their six children were lined up, along with Eric. A Russian officer shouted with the help of a translator: "Your names and nationalities!" "Herr Springle, Polish," replied the father, "Frau Springle, German," the mother hesitantly answered. The children gave their replies. Then it was Eric's turn. "I am Eric Armstrong, British Prisoner of War serving with the Royal Inniskilling Fusiliers." Suddenly the Russian officer pulled the gun from his holster and handed it to Eric. "These are your captors - shoot them!" he demanded. "No, no," said Eric, "I am not doing that, these people have been good to me." There was an awkward silence. The Russian officer paused for a moment and then replied, "Well, if you won't shoot them neither will I," and putting his gun back in its holster he walked away.

When the war ended and Eric was liberated, the Armstrong and Springle families were to become lifelong friends. In old age in his home in Armagh, reflecting on those dark days, Eric, strengthened in his faith by the experience, concluded that the Lord he trusted had brought him through and showed him that enemies can become friends. As I reflect on what happened those many years ago at the end of World War 2 and ask why Eric Armstrong was there, I think I know why.

Eric Armstrong

ALBERT THE NAZI AND THE MYSTERY NEW TESTAMENT

World War Two D Day landing

As we remembered the 70th anniversary of the D-Day Normandy landings on the 6th of June last, it brought back a personal emotional memory. It was 1975 that I visited the German City of Heilbronn. I was there with some Irish young people to do some mission work with German Christians on the streets of the very beautiful rebuilt city that had suffered the ravages of World War two bombing.

My immediate observation was to witness the enthusiasm and commitment of these German Christians. On the first day I was introduced to Albert, one of the local Methodist ministers, who was then I guess aged in his early sixties. He was charming and distinguished. Indeed he radiated a deep Christian experience. I felt I wanted to talk with him to get to know him better, although he spoke only a little English, but enough to be understood. One night as he drove me to my accommodation, he said suddenly in hesitant English, "Jim, I have something to tell you, and I am quite ashamed of it. I was a Nazi and a member of Hitler Youth. I fought in World War two.

Indeed looking back I am ashamed of many German Christians for not standing up to Hitler." There was silence, and then he went on to tell me that he had been deeply impressed by Adolf Hitler and believed firmly in the principles he propagated, so much so that he joined Hitler Youth.

With some emotion he concluded, "In the war I was captured by the Russians and

Berlin

spent some time in a Prisoner of War Camp. It was there that I received a New Testament, which I had never seen before. It had been smuggled in. I read it every day until one day I was so overcome by what Jesus did on the cross that I surrendered my life to him. When I left the camp I felt the call to full time ministry, so here I am. I am sorry for what we did." It was a deeply moving moment.

I have often wondered who that smuggler was. Did they ever know the impact it had on Albert's life? How important that person is in God's scheme of things! It was life changing and a testimony to the word of God in Scripture, that so often without any further explanation can be life changing to the one who reads it.

TERMINUS

When I was a wee lad, going occasionally to Bangor on the train was really something however my mother preferred Glengormley as I think it must have been a cheaper option. She would walk me to nearby Carlisle Circus in North Belfast where we would get a trolleybus. These buses ran on electric overhead cables and had a special kind of hum as they ran along the road. In those days there was nothing much to see at Glengormley but there was a rather quaint little ice cream shop. After a lick at the ice cream cone and a walk for about half an hour, we would return home. I was always fascinated by the conductor, who seemed to have only two things to say on any journey. One was "Fares please", and when we arrived at Glengormley village, he would should loudly, "Terminus!" That was a big word for me in those days. I reckoned it meant we had to get off. I didn't know then that the word terminus had a Latin origin. In ancient Rome, it represented both the boundary markers between properties and the name of the so-called god who watched over these boundaries. Nowadays we use it more loosely, sometimes to mean to cease, to stop, to end, or simply not to go any further.

I recall hearing a speaker describing some churches as having reached a terminus, because they were not moving on or growing. Their members were generally apathetic and lacking in enthusiasm. When I heard that, I contrasted it with the words of Luke writing in the Acts of the Apostles. Describing the early Church after Pentecost he says, "And they continued steadfastly *(no stopping or terminating)* in the apostles' doctrine and fellowship, in the breaking of bread, and in prayers." (Acts 2-42). These factors were the secret as to why the early Church grew.

While there are other factors that can cause the demise of a church, I would suggest that often churches that have reached the terminus have neglected those basic principles of prayer, study of the Scripture, attendance at the Lord's Supper, and the sharing with each other in meaningful, caring, loving fellowship. For 1st century Christians, reaching others with the good news of the gospel was a priority - consequently the Lord added to their number on a daily basis. It will not be the church building or the state-of-the-art premises that will positively change the future, but rather the same empowerment of the Holy Spirit that shaped the first Christian Church.

Finally, to those bus conductors who pulled the bell on the trolley buses and shouted "Terminus!" thanks for the memory. Over 50 years later it makes me think of that word in a different but much more profound kind of way.

Trolley Bus 1950's

NOT KNOWING SHE WAS RICH!

I read an interesting story recently about a lady living in a small European town. Her son decided to leave his impoverished conditions, and went to America where he became a successful and affluent businessman. A friend visiting his mother one day observed the spartan conditions she was living in, and asked her if her son ever sent her any money. "The only thing he ever sends me is pictures," she said. "But I don't need pictures, I need money." The lady then lifted a book where she had filed these so-called pictures. To the amazement of her friend the pictures were in fact American dollars, sent over an extended period of time by her son.

Now I wouldn't have made that mistake. I would certainly recognise an American dollar! But my life experience has taught me to appreciate the many things whose worth I have not recognised. I can think of my school days when I took little interest in my education and wasn't the best behaved or most conscientious pupil – something I had to make up for in later life.

I have been unwell on several occasions, and having been diagnosed with the neurological condition myasthenia gravis, I have come to understand the saying "your health is your wealth". At a material level on a visit to a shanty town in a third world country I recall the shock of seeing real poverty, not on a television screen but up close. It taught me to appreciate how well off I am.

Truly the woman who mistook the dollars for pictures would have enjoyed a better lifestyle if she had discovered their value. Yet perhaps she may have remained poor in the things that are of greatest importance.

A quote I read recently stated that if the only thing you possess is money, then you are poor. You are truly rich when you possess something that money cannot buy: to be loved by someone and to have an experience of the presence of God in your life. To know His grace and forgiveness, and the incomparable sense of joy that comes from knowing Jesus Christ, alongside the confident expectation of eternal life: this will do more for us than what any dollar bill can buy.

TALKED OUT OF IT

We met at a local cricket match. This stranger and I conversed at length with only one eye on the game. I offered him a lift, and when arriving at his home he said, "I am sure my wife would like to meet you." Soon the tea was provided. Within a few minutes of conversation my friend revealed my profession to his spouse. There was a moment of silence. Then came the question, "Do you know the Rev Sydney Callaghan" she enquired. He was a colleague of mine, I responded. There was an awkward pause. "Oh, then you know him." Her face gave nothing away and I wondered what was coming. I made no further comment and took the conversation in a different direction. On leaving, she looked me straight in the eye, pointed, and

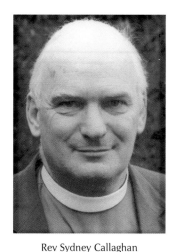

in a determined sort way said, "I would be dead today if it weren't for him, and have never got round to thank him." Sensitively I nodded and asked no further questions.

As was expected, I would meet my friend again in the usual place on the boundary. Our relationship developed and we became good friends. One day he said to me, "You remember my wife's remarks about your friend Sydney. I'll tell you what that is all about." He went on to explain the traumatic and horrific life of a young teenage woman who was eventually to become his wife. "She was going to take her own life, but she always said Sydney talked her out of it."

Rev Sydney Callaghan

I often thought of those words "Sydney talked her out of it". I knew well that there was just a slight inaccuracy: my guess was Sydney helped that young woman talk herself out of it. With the skills of a great counsellor, who often described himself just as a listener, he would have enabled her to identify the problem, see the reality of it all, and find light at the end of the dark tunnel. In a community in which suicide among young people has become a grim reality we need more Sydneys. I don't think he ever knew much more about the woman who became a wife, a mother and granny, nor that that time of listening was a turning point in her life.

My friend and his wife are now a long time deceased. I recall being at her funeral service and hearing those words of Jesus read: "In my Father's House". I could only smile and think well, if that's where she is I guess she has had a chance to thank Sydney.

A LICENCE FOR A CHIP SHOP

My father had a friend called Billy Haire who lived up the street. Billy's house was classy, it had carpet on the floor. We only had oil cloth, lino came later. Billy was a nice man, a devout Christian and an active member of Ebenezer Gospel Hall on the Oldpark Road in North Belfast. He was a bit of an entrepreneur, although he didn't enjoy good health and died as a relatively young man. He and his wife wanted to open a chip shop on a street between the Shankill and Crumlin roads. However Billy needed a bit of advice on how to go about this. He decided to seek the help of my father who had a reputation for being "in the know." My father told him that he needed to get a licence from the Belfast City Council before opening a business of this kind. He suggested that there might be an opportunity soon to speak to a city councillor. The following Saturday they trooped down to the Belfast City Hall dressed in their best.

Soon after they arrived the Lord Mayor, then one of Belfast's aristocracy, appeared fully chained and robed to switch on the Christmas tree lights. My father saw his chance, stopped him in his tracks and said, "Excuse me Lord Mayor, could you advise this man on how he might get a licence to open a chip shop?" The Lord Mayor was not amused and abruptly retorted, "Don't mind me saying but you could have picked a better day to enquire about a licence for a chip shop." Well I guess the Lord Mayor had a point, my father hadn't chosen the most appropriate moment, but it does remind us how difficult it is to gain access to the great and the good.

What always interests me is that the most important person of all, Jesus Christ, is available on 24 hour call all the days of our lives. We don't even have to wear our best gear, pretend we are terribly nice or put on a posh accent to approach Him.

The words of Banbridge man Joseph Scriven come to mind:

"What a friend we have in Jesus, all our sins and griefs to bear,
What a privilege to carry everything to God in prayer.
Oh what peace we often forfeit, oh what needless pain we bear,
All because we do not carry everything to God in prayer..."

The writer of the Book of Hebrews also reminds us how approachable God is, with these words: "Let us then approach God's throne of grace with confidence, so that we may receive mercy and find grace to help us in our time of need." Hebrews 4:16

Old Park Road Belfast

OVER THE TOP WITH A LASTING IMPRESSION

Sybil Megahey was an incredible woman who lived into her 90s. She was always very engaging. Born at the beginning of the 20th century in the Co Wicklow village of Tinahely, her stories of Ireland before partition were always informative and fascinating.

Sybil Megahey

In her east Belfast home one day she told me a story about her brother George that I will never forget. When he was enlisted into the British Army to fight in World War 1, she vividly remembered him kissing her goodbye as she played in the corner of the living room. George would never return home, as a telegram in the autumn of 1917 would inform his family that he was 'missing presumed dead' at Passchendaele.

Sybil's lasting memory of him was how he said a prayer with her the day he left home for the last time. She also remembers the terrible sadness in the family and the neighbourhood at the news of his death.

She then explained to me the amazing sequel to the story. Several years had passed, when one day a stranger arrived at the family home. He introduced himself as Bertie and then described his last memory of George who was his Sergeant. In the trench he recalled George removing a pocket testament from his uniform and beginning to read to his men. He spoke of his assurance that whatever happened in the days ahead, he would be completely trusting in Jesus Christ for the future, and he urged his men to do the same. Bertie described how when they went over the top, he got separated from George and was never to see him again.

The memory of George reading the scriptures that day so impressed Bertie that it was a turning point in his life. Bertie survived, but George, as Sybil said, "never returned." His body was never recovered and no grave marks his memory. As for Bertie, he explained to the family that as result of that experience he had committed his life to the Lord, and was now a full time evangelist travelling all over the country sharing the good news of the Gospel.

In recent years as we revisit the awful events of 1914-1918 I will be ever thankful that Sybil lived to tell me this remarkable story. As for Sybil, George, and Bertie they have now won the final victory that no grave can defeat.

WHEN FRIENDSHIP MAKES A DIFFERENCE

Irvinestown County Fermanagh

I still remember the first day I put my foot in the Co Fermanagh town of Irvinestown. This city boy was in for a shock. This pristine tidy little market town was some contrast to the drab streets of inner city Belfast where there was growing tension, with many areas scarred by civil strife. What could I expect from this town ten miles from the Donegal border? News coverage would also alert me to the dangers of living around here. Already people had been killed and murdered in these border counties.

On that lovely summer day in June 1972, I was to meet two people who would become lifelong friends. Douglas and Kathleen Hudson had a bakery and grocery business in the town. As this young rookie minister with wife and three year old daughter tucked into a sumptuous salad tea, I had some questions to ask. Soon I was to learn that the Protestants and the Catholics lived side by side on the Main Street.

A remark about how the two communities got on together in the town brought a straightforward answer from Douglas, almost with a slight rebuke: "We are not two communities here, we see ourselves as one community." I learned that Douglas was one of the town's trustees. He explained that they were made up of fifty percent from each side of the house. Power sharing I thought, before it had ever been invented.

What were we to learn from living in this town for the next six years? It was that the hand of friendship and the

Douglas Hudson

willingness to show respect broke down barriers. Douglas was the true Wesleyan Methodist, 'the friend of all and the enemy of none'. In the midst of those early days of the troubles I witnessed remarkable things happen. The 12th of July would come to the town and the G.A.A. Club would readily allow their car park to be used as the starting point for the Orange march. It would be trouble free. And the pipe bands from both traditions would lend each other drums for their big occasions. When I would conduct a funeral at the Methodist Church the whole community would gather.

Kathleen Hudson

After many years reflecting on it all I recall how people like Douglas made a difference in that small Fermanagh town. Every day he sought God's direction for his life. Like the famous evangelist Billy Graham he would read the Bible every day alongside the newspaper as he prayed for people in the town by name. But what strikes me more about him and Kathleen was the friendship they offered, never on the basis of religion or standing in life. Rich and poor were welcomed. No person came to live in the town of Irvinestown without an invite to their home, with a listening ear and an encouraging word, and most of all a welcome. When I left this peaceful town in 1978 to work for the next twenty-one years in east Belfast through the worst years of the troubles, I thought of those words of John Wesley:

"Do all the good you can, by all the means you can, in all the ways you can, in all the places you can, at all the times you can, to all the people you can, as long as ever you can." Douglas and Kathleen certainly fulfilled that commitment.

Billy Graham

BOBBY'S MUDDY HANDS

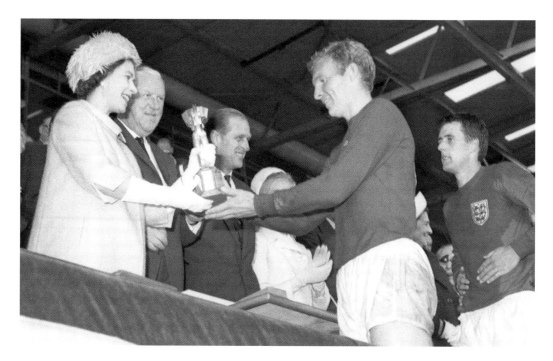

Bobby Moore with the Queen

I always live with the withdrawal symptoms of the World Cup. For four weeks every four years, I watch as many games as I can. I experience the typical "Norn Ireland" attitude of not supporting England in the early games, but living with the ability to transfer my allegiance if they get to the finals. I love to watch the World Cup not only for the games but for the memories. I recall the great 1958 performance of Northern Ireland in Sweden when all we had was the crackly radio commentary from Sweden. Things changed when we were able to witness the great performance of 1982 live on colour TV, the highlight being when Northern Ireland beat Spain in that famous win. But I suppose my abiding memory is sitting in my Uncle's wee house in west Belfast in 1966 watching England win the World Cup, and it seemed good even on a 14 inch black and white TV.

Some time ago a columnist Howard Long, writing in the Methodist Recorder, reminded us of 1966 and of watching Bobby Moore the England captain walk up the steps at Wembley to receive the Jules Rimet Trophy. He looked awkward as he kept wiping his muddy hands on his shorts. He was obviously concerned that a few seconds later he would shake the hand of the Queen. It was an understandable matter for embarrassment. He would not want to soil the white gloves of the Sovereign.

Yet in contrast one is reminded of the condition necessary to meet the King of Kings, God Himself. The psalmist asks, "Who may ascend the hill of the LORD? Who may stand in His holy place? He who has clean hands and a pure heart." (Ps.24) While that kind of purity is underlined by the psalmist David, he writes on another occasion of himself as a sinful man, and declares that he knows a God who can give him a clean heart and wipe out his sins with amazing forgiveness. The Bible never suggests that God gives merit to those who are good. St Paul says, "Christ died for the ungodly."

I am sure if ever we get the opportunity to meet the Queen, like Bobby Moore we would want clean hands. However it is good to know that the King of all Kings receives repentant sinners and makes them pure by His grace, all because of what Jesus did. The famous Methodist hymn writer Charles Wesley puts it this way, in the language of the 18th century, yet in words that are still commonly sung:

> He breaks the power of cancelled sin,
> He sets the prisoner free.
> His blood can make the foulest clean;
> His blood avails for me.

It assures us that we can come to God with muddy hands that He might make us clean, fit to serve Him and ready to meet Him in the life to come.

Northern Ireland v Sweden 1958

"ME MA."

Sarah Houston

It was in the late 1970s that I met Sarah Houston but I knew her better as "Harry's Granny." Harry was a mechanic who fixed my car and was a close friend. It was the death of her husband that began my acquaintance with Sarah. Mary, her daughter, referred to her in Belfast parlance as "me Ma". Sarah was a tiny woman, but quite opinionated in her own way. She had come through two world wars, had experienced sadness in her life and like many Belfast women of that generation Sarah had worked hard to support her family.

One day in conversation we talked about being a Christian and what it really meant. Sarah had her own thoughts which she expressed strongly. To put it her way, "Jim, I don't do anyone any harm, I always tried to bring up my family the right way and I'm good to my neighbours." However, I explained to her in what I hoped was a gracious way, that there was more to becoming a Christian than this. As we talked I am not sure exactly what I said, but I do remember we prayed. The following Sunday Sarah was in church. Not long after, she told me that she now believed the gospel and was a follower of Jesus.

Moving on from east Belfast I lost contact with her, but was delighted to hear that in the summer of 2005 she celebrated her 100th Birthday. One day I heard Sarah was dying and I went to see her. Mary her daughter met me at the door, "You've come to see me Ma," she said. Sarah I realised had been confined to bed for some time. She was blind, almost completely deaf, but as we say in these parts, "her mind was as sound as a bell." As I entered the bedroom, Mary shouted several times and could have been heard at the other end of the street. "Here's Jim Rea to see you, Ma." Suddenly from the bed a hand came forward to shake mine, and then these memorable words, "Many years ago you came to my house in Newcastle Street. We were talking about Christianity. I said I don't do anybody any harm; I live a good life and look after my family. I remember you said, 'Sarah it's not enough. It is not what you have done, it is what the Lord has done for you,' and that day I trusted the Lord Jesus Christ as my Saviour."

I was deeply moved; Harry's granny as a woman in her 80s, had discovered the wonderful simplicity of the gospel of the grace of God in Jesus Christ. She had witnessed to that experience for over twenty years. Not many days later Sarah at 102 years old was called home. I was privileged when asked to offer a tribute at her funeral service. It wasn't a problem! She was now in the Father's House having made the great discovery that it was not what she had done, but what Jesus Christ had done for her.

Happy birthday Ma

ENA'S KNITTING

The phone call was about Ena, a woman I knew very well. "Mummy's gone at last," said her daughter. It wasn't a shock for she had had a long protracted illness. I had known Ena for well over thirty years. She was a great woman in many ways. For years she volunteered in the East Belfast Mission's Homeless Centre, Hosford House. With knitting needles on her lap and a ball of wool that often got unravelled and rescued, she would sit for hours with men and women who had hurt and sadness in their lives, just listening and offering a quiet word of advice when needed. She understood people's problems. Life had been tough for her as a young woman; she had lost her husband to cancer and had to bring up her young daughter alone, something she did without complaint, laying down a good foundation.

Later that day I called to see her daughter Glynis and her family. "Your mum was always knitting," I said, "what kind of things did she knit – cardigans, socks?" Suddenly in the midst of the tears there was laughter as she replied, "You'll find this funny, Jim, but she never finished anything. There's wool everywhere and not a thing to show for it." I could hardly believe it. Three days later speaking at her funeral I said to the congregation, "Did you know about Ena's knitting: she never finished anything?" There were smiles and a few titters all round. Making my way to the cemetery I was listening to a news bulletin; an interviewee referred to "a work in progress" as he described his attitude to a forthcoming contentious parade. A bit like Ena's knitting, I thought!

A day before her death, I had watched the parade to mark the Centenary of the Ulster Covenant, the sun shone over Belfast, as many people obviously enjoyed the day in what was a relatively peaceful atmosphere. Earlier in the week I was aware that some Christians had walked the route, in silent prayer. I also knew that politicians, community workers, clergy, Orangemen and many others had worked tirelessly into the wee small hours to find a resolution. Yet even with all the efforts people remained anxious. Like knitting it might unravel. As people made their way home, I heard a sound bite on the radio: "The parading issue is not finished, there is much more work to do." Is anything ever finished? I thought. Then I recalled the words of Jesus spoken on the cross, "It is finished," which literally means paid in full. For on that day the work of salvation was completed. It was not our doing but God's.

I also remembered that Ena many years ago had a life-changing experience. She discovered what Jesus had done for her on the cross and had personally received the benefits of the new covenant that God alone can give, which is the forgiveness of sins, reconciliation with God, power to overcome our weaknesses, and life with Christ for evermore. She needn't have worried too much about the unfinished knitting.

MORE THAN A BREAD SERVER

As a student for the ministry I was fairly strapped for cash, so a summer job was necessary. In 1968 I secured employment with the Eglinton Bakery, based in West Belfast. The man in charge told me that because I was a student minister, he thought he could trust me with the takings. What I was to learn in the next few months should have been worth additional credits to my theological education. At 5.00am I would head out in the van for a long day. The deal was, I would go around with a bread server for two weeks and then take the reins for the next fortnight while he was on holiday.

One bread server I worked with, Hamie, stands out in my memory. Our run took us down a section of the Ards Peninsula, with an early morning stop at Newtownards to pick up newspapers - mainly the Irish News and the Newsletter. On my first day with Hamie, as we weaved our way down a country road, he remarked: "Now this is where the Newsletter ends and the Irish News begins." With due respect to the highly esteemed papers, I got the message. On those long drives through the winding roads of County Down we would talk. It interested him that I was training to be a Methodist minister and he would ask me endless questions. With a bit of a laugh one day, he confessed to being a Presbyterian.

As the days passed, I observed Hamie as he conversed with his customers. "You'll be getting the sash out for the twelfth," he would say, to one wee man who was all smiles. Further down the road, being shown a photograph of a young girl in her confirmation dress, he would remark, "Look at Bernie! Isn't she lovely." He was also up-to-date on the local G.A.A. He certainly moved a good few buns, as well as loaves. My initial impression was that he was simply a good salesman, and that he certainly was, but he was more than that, he was a man who showed respect for people, whatever their tradition or background, and he took a genuine interest in their lives.

Hamie was not an evangelist or someone who spoke about the Christian faith, but he taught me an important lesson: building relationships with people and showing a genuine interest in their lives, irrespective of who they are or where they come from and this is a quality to be desired by every Christian. I also often wonder whether if most people in Northern Ireland in 1968 had been like Hamie, we would have faced the thirty years of carnage that followed?

THE MAN WHO FIXED THE CHOIR

Billy Thompson

It was Sunday morning and we were doing a BBC radio broadcast service from our church in east Belfast. From an early hour that day all of those taking part were at the rehearsal. The soloist was Billy Thompson.

Billy was an east Belfast man. He would often talk unashamedly of his working class roots and his tough early life growing up in the poverty-stricken pre-war period. He was a real character and never short of an opinion. A gifted musician, he had amongst his talents a wonderful tenor voice and an incredible ability to motivate people to sing. He was in constant demand and was the conductor of several well-known choirs. His early Christian influence was in Pitt Street Methodist Mission Hall where the working classes and underprivileged found a welcome.

In the 1950s Billy left Belfast and for a time, went to Canada to work. It was there that he had a life-changing experience. One evening in the Peoples Church in Toronto he heard the renowned preacher and writer Oswald Smith. Billy experienced the grace of God in Jesus Christ and was converted. He returned to Belfast and joined Newtownards Road Methodist Church, now the East Belfast Mission.

He always felt that as a choir conductor he would not interfere with the local church choir. However on the morning in question we were in big trouble. At the pre-broadcast rehearsal the producer slipped in to the church. He said to the choir, "Please sing it again," and then called me out into the outside broadcasting studio. "I want you to listen to them," he said. "They are not good enough to go on the air. I suggest you just add an extra hymn."

I listened and realised he was being gracious - they sounded like a saw mill in full swing. However, I was worried; I didn't know how to let them down softly. I reflected for a minute and returned to the church. "Billy," I said, "the producer doesn't like the choir." Then I put the question, "Billy, we haven't got long, but could you give them fifteen minutes of your time?" Hesitantly he agreed. I said to the producer, "Give us a few minutes." Billy swung into action, rearranging the choir. He then quickly put the various sections over their parts. Suddenly a smiling producer returned to the church. "What's happened to the choir? They are transformed!" he shouted excitedly. I pointed to Billy. When it came to the broadcast, the choir delighted everybody with their singing.

The man who fixed the choir knew that God in a much more wonderful way had 'fixed it' for him. The night before his passing he quoted to me St Paul's words, "The time of my departure is at hand. I have fought the good fight, I have finished the course."

I often remember Billy Thompson with his lovely tenor voice singing gospel music, and I will never forget the day he fixed the choir. While honoured in life by Her Majesty the Queen, Billy has now gained life's greatest honour.

Shipyard cranes

THE IMPACT OF A GLASS OF MILK

Who would ever believe that the offer of a glass of milk would lead to such an amazing consequence! I read recently of a young American medical student walking through a rural area of Pennsylvania. It was a very warm day, and he was so thirsty that he stopped at a farmhouse and asked for a glass of water. A young girl came to the door, smiled and said, "I will give you a glass of milk if you wish." He drank the cold milk and went on his way refreshed.

Many years later he became a skilled surgeon. One day a patient was admitted to hospital. She was ill and required urgent surgery. It was the USA and, unlike our NHS, all treatment needed to be paid for. After the operation the young woman recovered well, but not being a person of means, she was apprehensive about the cost of her surgery. Prior to her discharge, she hesitantly asked for the bill. On it was a detailed account of all the procedures and at the bottom there was a total figure of the cost. But suddenly she was taken aback when she saw the following: "Paid in full with a glass of milk," and signed "Howard Kelly". Amazingly after many years the surgeon had recognised her name and address and this was an expression of his gratitude.

That famous doctor was Howard Atwood Kelly, one of the "Big Four" founding professors at the Johns Hopkins Hospital in Baltimore, Maryland. Dr Kelly was also a devout Christian and a trustee of the famous Moody Bible Institute. I consider it is more than speculation to suggest that the famous surgeon had some familiarity with the words, "paid in full." On the cross Jesus said, "It is finished." The Greek word he used was "tetelestai", a word used commonly in the ancient world on a legal document, or on receipt of payment, to mean "paid in full." Howard Kelly would have known the meaning of that word in the deepest possible way. He knew that Jesus had paid the price for his sin on the cross. I am not sure if he ever explained to the young woman why he had used these words to sign off his account. Perhaps remembering her kindness and filled with gratitude for the grace of God, that day Dr Kelly's generosity was compelled by the love of Christ.

Pennsylvania

"A METHODIST MINISTER ON THE MOON!"

On the 20th and 21st of July 2019 was dominated by the 50th anniversary of the moon landing. I thought where was I? I don't quite know where I was at 2.56am on 21st July 1969 when Neil Armstrong landed on the moon and echoed those forever famous words, "That is one small step for man, one giant leap for mankind." I certainly watched it, my memory suggests on an old black and white television with my late father.

What I have a greater recollection of, was what happened the following Sunday. I was a student minister and was working during the summer at the Belfast Central Mission, commonly known as the Grosvenor Hall. The Superintendent was the well known Rev Dr Eric Gallagher, and on Sunday afternoons with a group from the Mission he went to the Custom House Steps, then "Belfast's Speakers' Corner." A small group of men would gather to ask controversial questions or sometimes just banter and heckle. The speaker, (Eric as I came to know him) was well up for the challenge and usually got them off on a controversial note. On Sunday 27th of July 1969, he began as I best recollect, "I want to take issue with the President of the United States, Richard Nixon, who on hearing the news of the moon landing earlier last week, went on to describe it as the greatest moment in world history, since creation. Not decrying great scientific advancement, the statement is completely wrong and objectionable," Eric Gallagher insisted, and made the point, "The greatest moment from the creation of the world is when Jesus Christ put his foot on this world and God became one with us. It is called the incarnation."

Eric Gallagher's remarks that day was the first occasion I ever heard these sentiments expressed, and while I have read similar comments from many religious apologists about the Moon landing, I credit Eric as the first person I heard make this vital point.

The crowd were more subdued that day as the speaker expounded on what the coming of Jesus Christ to earth as God in human form really meant. It brought the possibility of forgiveness, a new world order called the Kingdom of God, and the confident hope for future life. It provided an example of how we should live our lives in Northern Ireland. I recall there were few questions, it was more civilised than some other days that I had been present. I guess they would have been more concerned had they heard that the Pope was landing on Sandy Row or that King William was landing on the Falls Road, than the Moon landing or the coming of Jesus Christ to earth.

Just a few weeks later in August 1969 Northern Ireland was not to take a small step but a giant leap into what was to be thirty years of mayhem, violence and murder.

Eric Gallagher lived for a further 31 years, until a few days before the new millennium. Until then he sought not only to make the gospel heard but also practised. Eric's words that Sunday afternoon were immensely profound. The sadness being that Irishmen and women in large numbers did not take that message seriously. If they had, Ireland might have been a different place. Fifty years on the message remains the same. God, having made a giant leap in love and forgiveness in the coming of Jesus Christ, wants us to take that small step of repentance and faith. Thanks Eric for the memory.

BUY BOTH SIDES OF THE HOUSE!

In 1999 I was sent to be minister of Thomas Street Methodist Church in Portadown. That's how the Methodists do it! You go where you are sent. At that time Portadown was in the news for all the wrong reasons. The Drumcree impasse, with the Orange

Order protesting for their right to walk the contested Garvaghy Road, would often be first on the news. There was much disruption in the town. I was told by some friends that I was going to the most divided town in Northern Ireland.

However, I was soon to realise that my perceptions were somewhat off the mark. One of the church members was Albert. He had a naval background and bearing, always very smartly dressed. I soon realised that he wasn't behind the door in giving an opinion. I was never sure he agreed with some things I said from the pulpit.

On Saturday mornings I would usually go to a local newsagent to buy my morning papers. I noted from my earlier observations that the most pleasant lady who owned the shop was, as we say in these parts, 'from the other side of the house.' As I left the shop one morning with a bundle of papers under my arm, I met Albert.

He looked a bit stern. "I see where you're buying your papers," naming the lady owner. I guessed I was in for a mighty rebuke. So I was ready to defend my corner against any form of sectarianism. Putting his arm around my shoulder, he said, "Fair play to you, I do the same myself. I always buy both sides of the house and show no prejudice." I soon discovered that the majority of Portadown people embraced Albert's approach.

I should have known not to make a hasty judgment. Only the Lord knows our real motives and intentions, and first impressions are not always right. And better still a few years later Albert trusted the Lord and spoke openly of his faith in Christ before his call to be with Him He is now eternally with those who know and love the Lord from both sides of the house.

Acknowledgements

I wish to acknowledge the help I have been given in the production of this book. The early prompting came from a woman called Ruth who as a teenager heard me speak at her small church in rural Fermanagh with a few dozen others in attendance. Often I would use a story to illustrate a point in sermon. Ruth obviously remembered and often reminded me to produce a book. Later I would become a friend of the late Derick Bingham. I greatly admired Derick as an outstanding Christian communicator. We would often talk and share some stories. Derick would insist I publish them. However several experiences of ill health would dampen my motivation.

Derick Bingham and Jim Rea

I have had cardiac issues and suffer from myasthenia gravis a neurology condition. However after a chance meeting with Cedric Wilson the subject of a book came up. Cedric put a proposal to me that such a publication could be sponsored and that he would undertake the publication. The meeting I believe was not by chance and without his help this project might never have taken place. I am indebted to Cedric and to the trusts, business community and personal gifts that has made this book to be published in such a manner that all of the cost of publishing has been covered, enabling virtually all of the purchase price to be given to the nominated homeless charities.

I wish to thank to Julia Grier who spent endless hours editing the text and advising helpful changes.

I am indebted to my wife Carol who has been my best supporter and constructive critic. We are also blessed with a wonderful family.

During the dark days of the troubles I had opportunity to speak to many people some involved and some tragically victims. There is no reference to these encounters as they will always remain confidential.

I trust that in reading this book you will recognise my central conviction, the power of the Lord Jesus Christ to transform the lives of men and women. It is the experience of having a personal relationship with the Him that drives me on. In a world that's in a mess I remain an eternal optimist. I believe the promises of God that every sinner who repents receives forgiveness and is given the power of the Holy Spirit. God has purpose for everyone, if we find this we have found the ultimate that leads to a life to come where death, suffering, and pain are no more.

This good news is neither sectarian or denominational. I am proud of my own religious tradition. I owe much to Methodism. However I wouldn't cross the road to make you a Methodist but I would go the longest distance possible to introduce anyone to Jesus Christ.

That is why If anything in this book have raised issues with you, or you feel I could be helpful please feel free to contact me at wjimrea@gmail.com

IRISH TEMPERANCE
LEAGUE

In writing this book I want to acknowledge the support and encouragement of the Irish Temperance League, a Christian based organisation founded over one hundred and fifty years ago, which continues to support those in the frontline battle against drug abuse and alcoholism. Recent statistics inform us that in Northern Ireland almost three hundred deaths per year are exclusively attributed to alcohol abuse. This does not include the alarming use of illegal drugs resulting in tragic deaths. Several of the stories in this publication are about people who have overcome addiction to alcohol and drugs to find a new life in Christ. Working in ministry for over forty years I have had the privilege of seeing lives changed by the transforming power of God. This book tells some of those stories.

The Irish Temperance League regularly offers grants to organisations assisting people to overcome addictions, and also to those in the field of education. Considering the pressures of modern society I enthusiastically commend an alcohol- and drug-free lifestyle, and am pleased to enter into correspondence through my email address. I am also in contact with many organisations who can offer support to sufferers and their families.

About the author

Jim Rea is a retired Methodist minister. He was elected President of the Methodist Church in Ireland in 2003. He worked on the Newtownards Road in Belfast at the Methodist Church for twenty one years and 1985 founded the East Belfast Mission. In 1995 he was awarded an MBE for services to the community. Jim Rea has witnessed some of the most horrific events of the troubles in Northern Ireland and his ministry has been almost exclusively in areas of conflict where he has ministered to many victims. Attempting to bring an end to violence he engaged with the leadership of opposing paramilitary organisations. In 2014 his portrait featured in an art exhibition by Susan Hughes ' Quiet Peacemakers'.

In 1999 he was stationed in Portadown and was involved in mediation to diffuse the impass at Drumcree. In 2006 he came back to work at the Methodist Church on the Shankill Road. He has a strong pastoral commitment to people with addictions and in 1994 completed a dissertation relating to religious experience, and alcohol addiction, being awarded a Master of Theology degree from the University of Oxford. He has travelled widely as a preacher and evangelist and is a regular contributor on BBC Radio Ulster Thought for the Day, and Downtown's, Just a Moment. He contributes regularly to a religious column in the Belfast Newsletter. Jim is married to Carol, they have three married children and six grandchildren.

Jim and Carol with their grandchildren